TWENTIETH ◀ CENTURY ● DESIGN

FURNITURE

PENNY SPARKE

Bell & Hyman

For my mother

Published in 1986 by
Bell & Hyman Limited
Denmark House
37-39 Queen Elizabeth Street
London SE1 2QB

*British Library Cataloguing in Publication
Data*

Sparke, Penny
    Furniture. – (20th century design; 2)
    1. Furniture – History – 20th century
    I. Title   II. Series
    749.2′049   NK2395

ISBN: 0 7135 2630 0 (cased)
        0 7135 2633 5 (pbk)

Designed by Richard Crawford
Typeset in 9½/13pt Linotype CRTronic
Sabon Roman by TJB Photosetting Ltd,
South Witham, Lincolnshire, England
Colour separation by Positive Colour Ltd,
Maldon, Essex, England
Produced in Great Britain by
Purnell Book Production Ltd, Paulton, Bristol

Other books in the series:
CERAMICS

Forthcoming titles:
GLASS
FABRICS AND WALLPAPERS
ELECTRICAL APPLIANCES
OFFICE FURNITURE

*Cover: Vico Magistretti's 'Selene' chair in ABS plastic was developed for
Artemide in the early 1960s and finally manufactured in 1968.*

*Overleaf: Three versions of a side chair in chromed steel and leather by Yrjö
Kukkapuro for Avarte Oy from the early 1980s which combine simplicity and
ergonomic precision.*

CONTENTS

INTRODUCTION

"I saw on the pavement, in front of the shop of a furniture dealer, some armchairs, chairs, dressers, tables.... These things the sight of which awakes in us the sensations and feelings of distant childhood, took on a solemn, tragic, even mysterious aspect."

Giorgio de Chirico 1935

THIS book is about mass-produced domestic furniture and its relationship with modern society and culture. Furniture, particularly the pieces we choose for our homes, and grow up with, expresses complex meanings. The home is the most private of inhabited spaces – the focus for many of the psychological and social dramas we enact – and the pieces of furniture within it carry the full burden of that symbolic load. To tell the story of ordinary domestic furniture in any period (especially the current one) is not, therefore, a simple task. The process of furnishing a home is, nearly always, cumulative. Few people buy the entire contents of their domestic environment at one time, so items from several periods may, and usually do, co-exist in a single home. This creates a problem of an archaeological kind, in addition to the difficulties of understanding the meanings that these pieces carry with them.

While the social and psychological context which provides insight into these hidden areas is among the most important aspects of any analytical history of furniture, there are other crucial elements in the story, such as general changes in the structure of the industry, in technology and in culture. Any account of modern domestic furniture which does not balance the way it has been used against the story of its production is incomplete. The expansion of the furniture mass market and the rise of the modern furniture industry are two sides of the same coin.

Perhaps the most important point to make about modern furniture is that it has shown a simultaneous commitment to innovation and tradition. This basic characteristic is reflected throughout its history in this century. Because furniture has such a long history, stretching right back to the early days of civilization, it has become one of the more stable elements within our frenetically changing society. Thus, while one branch of its evolution reaches out to grasp the benefits of new technology and materials, and to reflect cultural change, another retains constant links with the past, re-affirming its role as a symbol of stability, security and social status. On the whole, this psychological role of furniture as a sustainer of conventional values expresses itself in the continued use of wood and other traditional materials, such as cane and wicker. It also leads to the perpetuation of certain furniture types such as, in this century, the three-piece suite. On the other hand the progressive aspect of furniture design is shown in the use of new technologies and materials.

Inevitably, furniture types come and go. While basic domestic types – in particular the chair, bed and table – have had long histories, others have emerged only to disappear again soon afterwards, according to the dictates of changing technology and taste. Among those which have come and gone again are the Victorian dresser (which has, however, been the subject of a recent revival); the wardrobe (although still a common feature of bed-sitting rooms and boarding houses); and, more recently, the gramophone, the wireless set and the cocktail cabinet. Many others, such as the large television console, have a limited life ahead of them, while still others are yet to emerge. The rules which dictate what stays and what goes are highly complex ones. The whims of fashion, changes in social patterns and behaviour, and advances in technology all have an influence, as do new directions in architecture. One of the most dominant themes in domestic furniture of this century is in fact, its need to adapt to smaller and smaller living spaces, and this has brought with it the need for flexible and multi-purpose pieces. (Small homes have, of course, always existed, but before this century their inhabitants very rarely bought new furniture – they depended instead upon inherited pieces and the second-hand market.)

The two main craft traditions in furniture are cabinet-making and chair-making, and these two are still the basis of much modern manufacture. A distinction is still made between 'carcase' furniture – i.e. pieces made on a basic frame to which doors and shelves are added later – and seating, which relates more directly to the human body. The separation is also demonstrated in the domestic setting, where those items which have no direct contact with the human body have tended to become part of the structure of the room itself, leaving the others free to take on a life of their own. Thus, while in a Victorian home the kitchen and bathroom still contained a number of independent furniture pieces – such as dressers, tables and wash-stands – in modern homes these are usually 'built in' and no longer count as items of furniture. They have also become increasingly rectilinear, while seating (in particular the chair) has been the subject of countless efforts at visual innovation, many of them highly expressive. It is for this reason that the chair has tended to dominate most discussions about modern furniture.

The question of how avant-garde ideas relate to mass-production furniture is another recurrent and crucial theme in this century. It was the Viennese architect, Adolf Loos, who maintained that furniture is essentially a conservative force until it is used as an art form, and then it becomes subversive. It was not until the end of the last century that progressive artists and architects included furniture in their project to re-align architecture with contemporary culture. Since then architects have continually succeeded in pushing forward both the aesthetic and the cultural limits of furniture. From the British Arts and Crafts Movement, to the work of the Viennese Werkstätte, to the De Stijl group, to the Bauhaus, to the Pop designers and the Post-Modernists, a furniture avant-garde has existed in this century experimenting with new ideas, new materials and new forms in order to bring furniture into line with cultural change. Most of its statements have been unashamedly artistic, radical, high-minded and, above all, exlusive. It is, after all, the essence of the avant-garde to be one step or two ahead of the rest of society.

These avant-garde manifestations (which form the starting point for many studies on modern furniture) are, however, very different from what the majority of people in the industrialized world have bought and used in their homes in the years since 1900. While this book concentrates on the latter, more ill-defined and under-researched area, the role of the avant-garde is important nevertheless, in establishing the major breakthroughs of this century, most of which are reflected, sooner or later, in furniture for the mass market. Without the work of men like Marcel Breuer and Alvar Aalto, many of the furniture items that define the modern domestic interior would not look as they do. Always in search of new markets and new styles, the furniture manufacturer has of necessity, become a magpie, borrowing from wherever he can. The avant-garde provides many of his models.

The avant-garde is not, however, the only force to have effected changes in modern furniture. Perhaps the most important impersonal forces are the economics of production and consumption, and the availability of new technologies and materials. The impact of plywood, for instance, which took the place of solid wood in the manufacture of much high-volume production furniture in this century has been enormous, dramatically altering the appearance of much modern furniture. With plywood the panels of carcase furniture can be much larger and, as the structural strength is in the panels themselves, the mouldings cease to be essential. This kind of development has produced both a constructional and an aesthetic revolution. Without the availability of new materials, many of the innovations of this century could not have occurred. Without Mannesmann's seamless steel tube, for instance, Marcel Breuer would have been unable to create the combination of strength, openness and lightness that characterized his radical designs in tubular steel.

Few real advances in modern furniture have, however, come out of direct experimentation within the area itself, but rather as spin-offs from other fields. The advances made in materials technology during the two World Wars, for instance, had many knock-on effects on furniture manufacture in peacetime. Likewise seating that was first developed for modern transport – trains, cars and aeroplanes in particular – has, in turn, influenced furniture for the home. Foam rubber, for instance, was used in car seating before it entered the domestic arena, and Pullman kitchens provided the perfect solution to the space problems in American apartments in the 1920s and 1930s.

The dualism between innovation on the one hand, and the conservative tendencies of the mass market on the other, has also been mirrored in the way the furniture industry has developed in this century. While it has mainly developed into a system which has a high degree of divided labour, mechanization and standardization, it has, in some areas, also retained handwork and a more craft-oriented approach. This sprectrum spans, at one extreme, furniture design in America (which was much quicker than Europe to adopt mechanization) and, at the other, the craft workshops of Scandinavia and Italy. Many countries, however, have opted for a compromise, combining mass production with a wide diversity of products and some handwork, particularly for finishing processes. Inevitably the larger factories have directed their products at lower and lower income groups in order to expand their markets and to develop production, while the craft-based industries have continued to aim their goods at a higher income bracket, emphasizing quality rather than competitive prices. Those countries which have established strong international reputations for modern furniture (such as Italy and Scandinavia) have, on the whole, been the ones to retain a craft basis for their furniture production and to cater for fairly affluent markets.

The thorny question of 'taste' also lies at the heart of modern domestic furniture. Perhaps more than in any other consumer item, except fashion, the style of furniture is of fundamental importance to its purchaser. Since the early days of the expansion of its market beyond the aristocracy and upper middle classes, mass produced furniture has tended to ape 'socially superior' styles, and its role as a proof of social status has grown. The fact, therefore, that traditionally the aristocracy inherited antique furniture from their forbears led to a strong emphasis on period styles and reproduction pieces among the new middle class market. The same thing can be seen even in the very cheapest furniture made this century although here the copying of period styles has been a matter of free interpretation rather than of accurate reproduction. It was only gradually, as a result of economic pressures, that more modern styles were produced by the furniture industry and penetrated the homes of people who were purchasing new furniture for the first time. In recent years, however, popular taste in furniture has become more diversified and many different furniture styles both old and new, co-exist at many levels of the market. Furniture manufacturers geared to a high level of standardization have had to revitalize their product lines and to deal with a wider range than ever before. At the same time the smaller, more flexible companies have flourished.

All these themes, and several more besides, provide the subject matter for this book which aims both to examine the key moments when events completely changed the course of modern domestic furniture, and to provide a more general picture of what was going on at 'street-level', where conservatism rather than innovation was usually the norm. While the main structure of the text is chronological – moving from the early period of furniture industrialization in the late 19th century up to the present day – it also focuses on events in specific countries to show how different national factors often led to quite different results. These developments should be seen not as isolated incidents, but as aspects of a growing international scene. As we move nearer to the present it becomes apparent that, with the development of mass communications, the influences are felt increasingly rapidly of one country upon another and of one sector of the market upon another.

The culture of modern domestic furniture is very rich. Today, numerous, essentially modern, styles exist alongside any number of models from the past all of which bring memories with them into the present. It is this ambiguous relationship with the past and the future which makes modern furniture such a fascinating subject and renders it worthy of a study all of its own. It is also, incidentally, what gives so many of de Chirico's paintings their dramatic impact.

Philippe Starck's 'President M' table from the mid 1980s.

PART ONE

THE BIRTH OF THE MODERN FURNITURE INDUSTRY (1860-1914)

THE first section of this book focuses on the period during which the mechanization of the furniture industry took place – i.e. the second half of the 19th century, and the first decades of the 20th century. It was during this time, also, that a mass market for furniture first emerged, initially in Great Britain and soon afterwards in the USA and Continenetal Europe. The mechanization of the industry came about as a direct result of an increased demand for furniture, the availability of new ways of working wood and the new power sources (first steam and later electricity) which could drive the developing machine-tools.

Furniture was not, however, among the first industries to mechanize its production. In Britain the heavier industries such as ship-building and the textile industry, were well ahead (wood-working machines, however, initially developed for the ship-building industry were used for furniture production soon afterwards). Neither was furniture the first requirement of the lower reaches of the new consumer society, although by the end of the 19th century, it was increasingly in demand. The main hindrance to the mechanization of British furniture production was the easy availability of cheap manual labour and the continuing efficiency of the division of labour system introduced some years earlier. Although some machines had been introduced by the 1860s, much handwork was also preserved and, in some instances, remained so for almost a century.

In the USA things were very different. The workshops established on the East Coast in the first half of the century and extended to the Mid West in the second half, were furbished with more advanced machine tools than their British equivalents. A company called Page and Co., for example, was set up in New Hampshire in 1834. Its founders had invented the foot-powered mortising machine and a tenoning machine and they drove them around in a wagon, selling them to the small woodworking shops in the area. By 1860 the wooden frames of these machines had been replaced by cast-iron and they had reached a high level of sophistication. In addition the American manufacturers had a vast, highly homogeneous market to supply, a large section of which needed pieces for the homes they were setting up in the 'New World'. American industrial organization was pioneered by the meat-packing, and pistol-production industries which had relied from the beginning upon the division of labour and standardized production. As soon as furniture production had developed on a reasonable scale these principles were applied to it likewise.

In general terms Continental Europe was slower than both Britain and the USA to mechanize its furniture manufacturing and to cater for a mass market, and it was more reticent to move away from upper middle class taste. The major innovations in Europe at the turn of the century were exclusive and avant-garde in nature, concerned more with the question of furniture style than with the process of manufacture. It was from France, Germany and Austria that the first 20th-century furniture style emerged, in the form of the movement called Art Nouveau or, in Northern Europe, Jugendstil. This did not hold sway over popular taste for long, however, and was replaced by a sequence of new furniture styles – many of them originating in Vienna – inspired by the simple modern forms which the Arts and Crafts Movement in Britain had done so much to popularize a few decades earlier. Little of this penetrated the mass market in a major way, however, and the European furniture industry remained preoccupied, on the whole, with period styles. A significant exception was represented by the work of the Austrian company, Thonet, which looked to American production models for

inspiration rather than to the firms in its own country of origin. Germany also responded to the American methods of mass manufacturing which it first came across at the Chicago World's Fair of 1893. As a result, experiments in modern furniture in that country were committed, early in the century, to the ideas of mass production and consumption.

The main emphasis in Europe in this period was, however, upon stylistic eclecticism, high fashion and the expression of social status for the expanding sector of the market which could afford to buy it. Among the most significant technological advances of the day were those made in the area of upholstery. While the earliest examples of the process date from Jacobean times, little had changed by the 18th century when armchairs were still stuffed with wool and horsehair. Victorian armchairs had, however, large coiled springs in their seats giving them extra resilience, thanks to the invention of a certain Samuel Pratt who patented the technique in 1828. Other technical advances of the day included the foray into metal furniture which never really caught on – except for the metal bed which took over from its less hygienic predecessors.

The other major furniture revolution of this period, which accompanied the arrival of mass production and consumption, was the way in

which it was retailed. This was the period when the department store and the specialist shop took over from craftsmen's showrooms. Credit buying was introduced for the less affluent and, as a result, more and more people bought new furniture, thereby making mass market furniture a reality for the first time. These were the years, then, in which mechanization began. Mass-produced furniture existed alongside the custom-made pieces which had long fulfilled the requirements of the aristocratic and upper middle class market. This amounted to nothing less than a major revolution in the way furniture was made, bought and used.

An advertisement for the Original Austrian Bentwood Company which appeared in the Cabinet Maker and Art Furnisher *in June 1882.*

THE ORIGINAL AUSTRIAN BENT WOOD FURNITURE CO.

Garden or Bar Sofa.

No. 14 Sofa.

Circular Table.

Bar or Office Stool.
18 in., 24 in., and 28 in.

Smoking Chair.

Ladies' Rocker.

Bar or Office Stools.

No. 14½.

Easy Arm Chair.

1

BRITAIN AND THE RISE OF THE MASS MARKET

IT wasn't until the middle of the 19th century that the majority of the British public could either afford, or had any interest in purchasing, new items of furniture. The twin forces of industrialization and urbanization created at that time an unprecedented demand for furniture on a mass scale. Suddenly there was an expanding population with more money than ever before to spend on goods other than the bare essentials of life. People were moving from the country to the city and needed to furnish new homes and, perhaps most importantly, social groups which had never purchased new furniture before, wanted to display their newly acquired wealth in the form of status objects in the home.

Until this time the acquisition of furniture had been for most people (as it continued to be for the poorest sections of the community) a matter either of inheriting from friends or neighbours, or of buying on the second-hand market. The purchasing of new furniture pieces had been restricted to the aristocratic and upper middle class sectors of society.

Now, with increased general wealth among the middle, and a section of the working classes, buying furniture became a much more common feature of everyday life and took on an increasingly significant role in British society.

Much furniture was, inevitably brought from the country to the town, and, as a result, great numbers of kitchen dressers and Windsor chairs appeared in Victorian interiors. Along with simple wooden tables and a few other basic items, they also provided the furnishings for many of the 'below stairs' areas of more affluent households. In the 1850s, most working class families furnished their homes in stages, either from the second-hand market or from the large furniture warehouses which provided them with cheap, heavy, wooden items. The furniture makers, based in Shoreditch and Bethnal Green, supplied these outlets with their goods and had to work hard to meet the ever increasing demands of the public in this period. Payment was usually made with the

help of credit and the kind of items that would be bought included, according to R. Roberts in his book *The Classic Slum, Salford Life in the First Quarter of the Century, "a leather sofa, a hardwood armchair, a hardwood rocking-chair, four kitchen chairs, a square table, a washstand with a tiled back and two cane seat chairs."* Together with a range of other household items this was thought to provide the complete set of furniture items suitable for the one-up, one-down house which so many of the new town-dwellers inhabited in the second half of the century.

By 1900, as a writer in a 1957 copy of the *Evening News* explained, the ordinary working family could furnish its entire house for £20 and the two items which brought it the greatest amount of social status were the marble-topped washstand and the over-mantel in the living room, which was always topped with a large mirror mounted in a carved wooden frame. Other essentials, according to this same account, included a 'black

A pair of Victorian balloon dining-chairs in walnut with upholstered seats and carved decorative details. Chairs such as these would replace the cheaper Windsor chairs of less affluent households.

and brass' bedstead; the inevitable Windsor chairs; and, for the more affluent only, a seven piece 'American cloth' suite which consisted of a settee, two easy chairs, and four small chairs. Few major changes took place in this furniture line-up for a number of decades, although an increasing number of households began to enjoy the benefits of living with it.

The crucial factor, apart from price, in the mass consumption of furniture at this time was the concept of 'taste' which influenced the choice of all but the very poorest families. The principle of 'upward emulation' was still widespread, inherited from the previous century when aristocratic values had been the ones which influenced all aspiring members of society. In her book *Lark Rise to Candleford*, for instance, the writer Flora

A typical middle class Victorian living-room from the 1860s. The profusion of ornamental detail, combined with the dark wood of the heavy furniture items, represented that class's search for a visual symbol of its newly-acquired opulence.

Thompson evoked the way in which domestic servants sought to emulate their employers' taste values in this description of the interior of one of her character's homes: "*Instead of the hard Windsor chairs of her childhood's home, she would have small 'parlour' chairs with round backs and seats covered with horsehair or American cloth*". Fashion became increasingly important to the new consumers who looked to the styles of the 'old consumers' for inspiration.

Where fashionable furniture was concerned, from the 1850s onwards popular styles moved from the bulky pieces and the eclecticism of the mid-century through to simpler forms and patterns inspired by the movement called 'Art Furniture' which dominated middle-class taste in the last three decades of the century. In 1937 the writer Christopher Hobhouse looked back to the furniture at the 1851 Crystal Palace exhibition. He described what he called the "*dreadful outburst of popular furniture*" which had been shown there, explaining that "*Popular taste has always preferred... the natural to the architectural... the 'people' demand that every table should point its moral and every chair should tell its tale.*" The highly carved and heavily upholstered pieces at the 1851 exhibition influenced popular taste for a couple of decades before they were replaced by the finer lines of the later

A Sussex chair of ebonized beech with a rush seat made by Morris and Company in about 1865 and inspired by Morris' interest in British country furniture.

century which owed more to Japan than anything else. In this change of emphasis the International Exhibition held in London in 1862 was of great significance. There was also in existence by this time, a more substantial lower middle class market ready to leap upon every new furniture fashion.

Apart from the Japanese-style 'Art' furniture introduced to the British public in 1862, the exhibition also served to bring to the public's notice the work of William Morris and his colleagues whose Arts and Crafts pieces owed much to Medievalism as well as to the British vernacular tradition. However loudly

Morris expounded his ideas about craftsmanship and 'good making' and his belief in the links between design and social revolution, nothing could prevent the furniture produced by his firm, Morris and Company, from becoming just another model for fashionable, middle class taste in the late 19th century. The power of the mass market was by now such that every innovation, however high-minded, became merely another source of inspiration for the popular style-makers. The publication of a number of books in this period, including Charles Eastlake's *Hints on Household Taste* of 1867, added fuel to this fire, and the new retail outlets – among them Liberty's in Regent Street, which dealt almost exclusively with items for the 'artistic' home – made the fashionable furniture pieces much more easily available, at least for those who could afford them.

At the cheaper end of the market the growing demand for new furniture was met by a number of specialist furniture retail outlets which set up business in the last decade of the century to cater for lower middle and working class tastes. One such shop was established by a certain John Jacobs who, in 1894, moved from running a small outfitters in the City to opening the 'Debtford Furnishing Company' in New Cross Road in London. The main reason for the success of his company was its commit-

A photograph of Morris and Company's dining-room interior for Stanmore Hall, which appeared in The Studio *magazine in 1893, thereby influencing the style of many other interiors in that decade.*

A page from a Liberty and Company Limited catalogue from the 1880s showing the kind of furniture items retailed by that shop to its predominantly middle class clientele.

Messrs. GREGORY'S STOCKS, on Sale by Liberty & Co. Ltd.

The TWO SETS OF PRICES show the REDUCTIONS made for the present CLEARANCE SALE.

Antique Furniture (continua).

Original Price. Sale Price.
£ s. d. £ s. d.

An old English Chest of Drawers with Shaped Front. Inlaid.
Height, 2 ft. 6 in. ; Width, 2 ft. 10 in. ... 10 10 0 ... 8 10 0

A Handsome old Carved Oak Cabinet with Folding Doors, top and bottom, and Six Drawers in the Centre. The panels heavily moulded with round and Diamond Shaped Ornament. Across the Top a Finely Carved Band with Coat of Arms, Amorini and Scrolls : 16th Century.
Height, 7 ft. 6 in. ; Width, 5 ft. ... 63 0 0 ... 42 0 0

A French Table, in Rosewood and Marqueterie, of fine workmanship. Cabriole Legs with Ormolu Mounts. Empire Period.
Length, 4 ft. 2 in.; Width, 2 ft. 4 in. ... 30 0 0 ... 21 0 0

Modern Furniture.

The following are Representative Specimens of this COSTLY and EXTENSIVE STOCK. It embraces the most EXCLUSIVE and ORIGINAL DESIGNS : and reproductions of the choicest examples of early ENGLISH, ITALIAN, and FRENCH Art. *All the specimens are of the most finished workmanship.*

Messrs. GREGORY'S STOCKS, on Sale by Liberty & Co. Ltd.

The TWO SETS OF PRICES show the REDUCTIONS made for the present CLEARANCE SALE.

Modern Furniture (Sideboards).

Original Price. Sale Price.
£ s. d. £ s. d.

Oak Sideboard, 7 ft. 6 in., handsomely Carved and Moulded ; shaped Front with Drawer and Cupboard below, Carved Panels and Pediment ... ... 115 0 0 ... 65 0 0

Spanish Mahogany Sideboard, 7 ft., elaborately Moulded, and with Finely Carved Ornamentation ; Straight and Angle Cupboards, Panelled Doors ; 4 Drawers, Cupboard in centre fitted with Cellarette ; Bevelled Mirrors and Cupboards in upper part for China ... ... 68 0 0 ... 45 0 0

Solid Oak Sideboard, 5 ft., with Carved Doors to Cupboards, Shelf on Top and Long Drawer in Centre ... ... 21 0 0 ... 13 0 0

Oak Sideboard, 5 ft. 6 in., with 3 Cupboards, and Sliding Trays for Plate in centre, Carved Door Panels, Bevelled Mirror in Back ... ... 20 0 0 ... 10 0 0

Mantel Fittings.

A Handsomely Carved Oak Mantel Fitting, 5 ft. 9 in., Bevelled Mirror in centre, Shelves, and Carved Pediment, Marble Slips and Tiled

ment, right from the very beginning, to accepting payments staggered over a period of time. This practice had, hitherto, been much more common in such durable items as pianos and sewing machines than in furniture. Its application to this new area led rapidly to a huge expansion in the sales of furniture pieces to the ordinary working family. Jacobs' company was later transformed into 'Times Furnishing' and became one of the best-known furniture retail outlets in British high streets all over the country by the second half of the 20th century.

One inevitable response to the increased demand for furniture in the second half of the 19th century in Britain was the expansion and reorganization of manufacturing. While it was not possible to speak of a full-scale industry in Britain until the arrival of electrification at the turn of the century, countless changes had taken place, both in the structure and methods of furniture manufacture, in the preceding decades.

A number of advances had already been made in the development of wood-working machinery since the end of the 18th century. Jeremy Bentham's invention of rotary cutting followed by Marc Isambard Brunel's famous block-making machine and his improvements to the circular saw were all discoveries aimed at improving the process of ship-building but had, inevitably, numerous benefits for the more traditional work of cabinet-making and chair-making as well. After these early British advances, however, the USA took up the challenge of improving wood-working techniques while Britain was slower to respond and lost its lead in this area.

What little British manufacturing innovation there was in the second half of the 19th century was focused in the furniture industry in High Wycombe which had specialized in the production of Windsor chairs and cheap cane and rush-seated chairs. Because it catered for the lower echelons, it could supply the vast proportion of the expanded market of the second half of the 19th century. While the major furniture-producing area until then had been London – in particular the East End and the area around Tottenham Court Road – High Wycombe now took over, and even enticed several London manufacturers – including Frederick Parker and Sons – to pack up and move there. It wasn't until the 1860s, however, that High Wycombe companies began to use steam power as the driving force for its increasingly specialized machines – among them the older circular saw, band saw and lathe, and the newer 'seat-borer' (which made the holes to take the chair legs), dowel-making machines and round tenoner machines. The

introduction of these machines by no means eliminated handwork, however. It simply reduced the number of errors that were made. Also no attempts were made to standardize production and a huge diversity of designs continued to emerge from the High Wycombe factories, as they had always done from the less mechanized London workshops. J. Cinnamon Limited of Hackney, for instance (established in 1908 to produce high grade chairs and settees) was said to have over 2000 models available, while an 1872 catalogue of a High Wycombe company called William Collins and Sons showed over 330 variations of Windsor and Wycombe chairs.

Along with the introduction of steam and, later, motor-driven machines, the High Wycombe firms also developed a more sophisticated division of labour system than before. A caned chair, for example, would pass through about a dozen hands before its completion. Outworkers were still used to quite a large extent as well so there were quite a variety of production modes working alongside each other.

Between 1885 and 1905 the number of furniture factories in the area rose from about 50 to about 100 and, inevitably, their output expanded enormously as well. By the turn of the century, however, there were signs that a number of the more

successful companies were moving away from the production of 'low-grade', traditional furniture pieces and towards items such as upholstered chairs, sofas and cabinet work. The move into the area of 'art furniture' was primarily a response to growing competition in the area of 'ordinary' furniture from the USA and Austria, whose industries expanded more quickly than Britain's in this period and operated, from the start, on a larger international scale.

These new pieces had to be differently retailed as the High Wycombe firms did not want their customers to know of the furniture's rural origins. As a result, several firms established their own showrooms in London. By the turn of the century, also, many of the large department stores and furniture specialists – among them Scholbreds, Maples, Whiteleys, Gillows and Heal's – were mass-producing their own furniture and selling it to a predominantly middle class market.

On the whole, however, while expansion and mechanization of the British furniture industry did take place on an unprecedented scale, this process was by no means comparable with the changes which occurred in the USA in the second half of the 19th century. Britain's furniture production remained part industrial, part craft for several decades and it wasn't until after the Second World War that this was to alter significantly.

2

TRADITION AND MECHANIZATION IN EUROPE

COMPARED with Britain, the Continent was slower in moving from craft to factory production. This can be explained by a number of factors, not least among them the fact that Britain's population expanded much more quickly than that of any other European country. In textiles, for instance (the first of the mass-produced consumer goods) France continued to make exclusive silks while Britain moved into the mass production of inexpensive fabrics such as calico – a pattern echoed in furniture production.

In addition, Continental society did not undergo the same dramatic changes as its British equivalent in these years. Urbanization and the mass market did not develop, generally speaking, for them until the turn of the century.

The skilled cabinet-maker, protected in many European countries by the guild systems which had remained unchanged for many centuries, was still the main producer of furniture which was aimed at a predominantly aristocratic and upper middle class market. These late developments were due primarily to the fact that many European countries did not, in fact, become independent nation states until fairly late. Germany, Italy, Scandinavia and Austria – all of them countries with strong modern furniture traditions – were all products of the late 19th and early 20th centuries. As a result they were relatively late in starting to build up their industries and in developing their mass markets. From the 1880s onwards, however, industrialization and urbanization expanded rapidly in countries like Germany and Austria, accompanied by a sharp rise in population figures and an improvement in the general standard of living. France, with its strong dependence on agriculture, and Italy with its lack of resources, lagged somewhat behind at this stage, however. As in Britain, the industrialization that took place in Europe at this time was concentrated in the 'heavy' areas of coal, iron and steel, and had relatively little impact upon the traditional industries, which continued to use long-established production methods. This was due to the fact that the dominant social values remained, for a long time, in the hands of the nobility and, later, the 'bourgeoisie' who emulated aristocratic taste as closely as possible.

Thus, even though in countries such as France real wages rose for much of the population, furniture production remained exclusive, craft-oriented and dominated by period styles. Describing goods for sale at the Bon Marché department store in Paris, for instance, the writer Michael B. Miller discusses the presence of what he calls 'deluxe cabinet work' in the 1870s. Much of it was made in the small workshops which Bon Marché gathered around it.

One major exception to this traditionalist tendency was destined, initially at least, for the commercial rather than the domestic market. Although the founder of the Thonet company, Michael Thonet, was Prussian-born he was enticed to Vienna in 1842 and it was there that he set up his furniture factory and first retail outlet in the middle of the century.

A Viennese interior by Oscar Strad from 1917 showing a richness of decorative detail characteristic of that period of Viennese interior design.

Thonet had already been experimenting with the processes of laminating and bending wood, and he opted in the 1880s for a manufacturing technique which involved bending solid beech attached to a steel strap. He was not the first to perfect the bending process – Windsor chairs had been made out of bentwood for some time – but he succeeded in turning his production into a large-scale, mechanized venture that could fulfil the needs of an international mass market.

The 1850s and 1860s were the decades in which the Thonet company expanded rapidly, opening a factory in Moravia in 1857 which employed no craftsmen or cabinetmakers, but rather a team of workers who co-operated on the tasks of cutting, bending and assembling the machine-made furniture. The process was rationalized to a very high degree and the production of the furniture was completely standardized. The Thonets even built all their own machinery, ranging from multi-blade saws to machines for bending the seats and legs. Handwork was retained for some processes, such as screwing the chairs together, but this was essentially unskilled work which could be taught fairly quickly. A major feature of Thonet furniture lay in its knock-down property which meant that, from the start, it was designed with foreign export markets in mind.

The simple chair number 14 and the B9 desk armchair which appeared in 1904 are among the best known of Thonet's pieces and have remained familiar items for many people through this century. Because of their realtively low price and their ubiquity in cafés, hotels, restaurants, and assembly halls, they have been able to sidestep the demands of 'ruling taste' and fulfil a much more utilitarian role. In his excellent monograph on the Thonet company, Christopher Wilk remarks that *"it was chiefly in the more remote export markets such as England and the United States that bentwood chairs were more commonly used in domestic settings and that was due, without doubt, to their high novelty value in those foreign settings."* The more ornate pieces – the rocking chair, the armchairs, tables and sofas – were more obviously domestic and were not produced in such great numbers. The rocking chair had a particular appeal in the USA – the country of origin of that particular chair-type – while in Europe it was considered 'suitable only for the sick and invalid'.

At the turn of the century the Thonet company began inviting a number of well-known architect-designers to provide it with new furniture forms, and it was through the Thonet company (as well as its competitor, J. and J. Kohn), that men like Adolf Loos, Koloman Moser, Otto Wagner and Josef Hoffmann designed their most 'public' pieces of furniture. While the anonymous bentwood items had been designed with both traditional and modern interiors in mind, the Viennese architects were committed to the idea of a new style for the new century and, to that end, they exploited the Thonet idea of simple, standardized forms. Loos' chairs for the Café Museum of 1899 and Hoffmann's pieces for the Café Fledermaus of 1905-7 bear witness to this tendency and remain among the most popular of this century's chair designs.

The idea of finding a new furni-

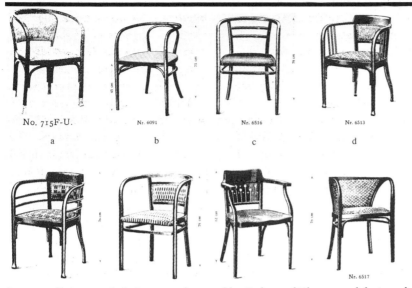

No. 715F-U.
a

Nr. 6091
b

Nr. 6516
c

Nr. 6513
d

Nr. 6517

A range of bentwood chairs manufactured by Kohn and Thonet and designed by the Viennese designers, Gustav Siegel and Otto Wagner, in the years between 1904 and 1911.

ture style which would counter the historic tendencies of the period was, at the turn of the century, a major preoccupation in European architectural and design circles. They based their search, for the most part, on the aesthetic and social ideals of the British Arts and Crafts Movement, with the same commitment to production by hand rather than machine. These avant-garde designers included Art Nouveau architects in Belgium and France (e.g. Gustave Serrurier-Bovy, Victor Horta, Henri van de Velde, Louis Majorelle, Emile Gallé, and Eugene Gaillard), Antonin Gaudi in Spain, the Werkstätte architects and designers in Vienna, and the group gathered around Charles Rennie Mackintosh in Glasgow. Their designs, however, failed to penetrate the mass market to anything like the extent of the Thonet chair.

The Art Nouveau architects and designers made their impact mainly through magazines. Some manufacturers did emulate the prototypes they saw in illustrations, but usually in a watered-down form and mixed together with other current stylistic influences, such as Aestheticism, Japonisme and the Arts and Crafts movement. Art Nouveau furniture and interior design failed to oust the ruling taste of the day, which was dominated by the Biedermeier style of interior decoration. It was also no match for the vast numbers of reproduction, second-hand and eclectic furniture pieces which met the needs of the largest sector of the European market. Such Art Nouveau furniture as was produced was cabinet-made, and, as Karl Mang rightly observes in his book on modern furniture, *"By the time furniture factories had begun to exploit the fashion, Art Nouveau had already passed its peak."* Unlike the Thonet brothers, the avant-garde European designers were not in tune (except intellectually) with the spirit of modern production. They had little idea about manufacturing practicalities, and only understood the needs of the most exclusive markets.

Cabinet-making remained the norm in most European countries for domestic furniture. It was either made to order or purchased from the large department stores. Apart from Austria, with Thonet, the only other European coutnry to move towards furniture for the new, expanding market was Germany. Since its independence as a nation state in 1871, Germany's joint programme of industrialization and urbanization had been executed more rapidly than in any other European country, save Russia. The population had also grown enormously and the wealth of the general public had risen appreciably. The new rich were packed densely into the major cities and numerous industries developed to meet their expanding material needs.

At the turn of the century, the craft workshop was still the dominant unit of furniture production, but moves were soon afoot to establish a standardized, mass production system. One example of a design initiative in this direction was the work of the Deutsche Werkstätten which was formed in 1907 and which soon had four furniture factories, in Munich, Bremen, Berlin and Hamburg. A branch of the Werkstätten was based in the new Dresden-Hellerau garden city. Two individuals associated with this group were Karl Schmitt (a cabinet-maker who had opened a furniture workshop in Dresden in 1898), and his brother-in-law, Richard Riemerschmid. Together they were determined to design a range of furniture which would combine cheapness with the possibility of mass production by machines, and they showed their first attempts at this venture in an exhibition in Dresden in 1905-6. Their furniture was aimed at the middle class client of limited means, and its main appeal was the way it combined a hint of fashionableness, in its Art Nouveau curves, with a simplicity and an 'ordinariness' similar to much vernacular furniture. Another member of the group, Heinrich Tessenow, concentrated on what he called 'simple, decent' furniture items which were

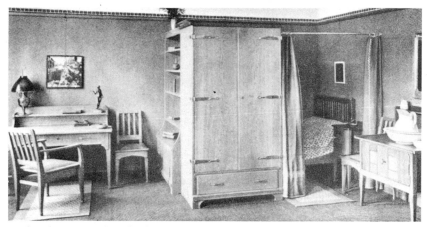

Richard Riemerschmid's design for a combination living/dining room of 1907 intended for the dwelling of a low-income family. While the stylistic idiom is Arts and Crafts the chairs were mass-produced from standardized components.

modestly priced. He used forms recalling country furniture, – which was still the most common possession of many of the families who had only recently moved into the new urban environment, – and his pieces suggested a bridge between craft and industry. In reality, however, while they were widely available, they tended to appeal to a more style-conscious audience than their originators had wished. Versions of Riemerschmid's simple chair were, for instance, sold through Liberty in London, a store which catered for a highly sophisticated clientèle.

Standardization of parts greatly interested the German group, who adopted the idea of 'Unit' furniture. This had originated in the USA in the production of bookcases, and it entailed manufacturing standardsized components which were then assembled in a number of alternative ways. The Werkstätten exhibited what it called 'typenmöbel' (furniture-types) in 1910, thus introducing to Europe a concept which was to become increasingly important as the mass production furniture industry finally gained a foothold.

By the First World War it was possible to speak about a real democratization of furniture in Europe, but nowhere did this challenge the massive scale achieved in the United States of America. It is there that one really sees how mass furniture styles could penetrate the majority of a population.

3

THE DEMOCRATIZATION OF COMFORT IN THE USA

"The development of furniture manufacture in the USA has closely paralleled the changes in social and industrial conditions since the Revolution and has in particular reflected the increase in wealth during the last half century and the accompanying greater attention to comfort and luxury in the home"
C.R. Richards 1922

THE same pattern of events that characterized both the growth of the mass market and the move from craft workshops to mechanized mass production in Britain and Europe, also occurred on American soil in the second half of the 19th century. The main difference was that in the USA they took place more quickly and on a much grander scale.

From 1830 onwards the American population expanded in leaps and bounds and during the next few decades the amount of its disposable income shot up beyond all expectations due to rapid industrialization all over the country. Mechanization penetrated American life more quickly than it did European, due to a number of factors – not least among them the lack of the cheap work force on which Europe depended for its manufacturing industries. Machines of all kinds changed the nature of work in both agriculture and industry in the USA and products like the mechanical reaper, the sewing machine and countless machine-tools helped speed up the mass production of food and manufactured goods.

The new market which emerged in the USA, ready to spend its newly-earned cash on products to guarantee it enhanced social status and bear witness to its material wealth, was both much larger and more homogeneous than its European counterpart. Manufacturers could rely on large sales for their products which meant they were able to invest in mass production of standardized objects, all made of interchangeable parts, and to equip their factories with all the specialized machines that they needed for this mammoth task.

Furniture was one of the first 'needs' of this new market and it quickly became apparent that the relatively small numbers of immigrant (mostly German) craftsmen who were engaged in the production of furniture would be incapable of fulfilling the demands of the new consumers. As a result an American mass production furniture industry emerged in the 1860s and, in terms of organization of labour and specialized mechanization, it developed rapidly into one of the country's most advanced manufacturing areas.

Early on, furniture production was centred on the East Coast, but in the mid-century, as the population moved further and further west, the industry became focused in a number of new areas. The Mid-West centres were ideally suitable. They could offer water for the steam-powered machinery, access to ready supplies of timber, and a central location. Chicago, Grand Rapids and Cincinatti allowed for easy transportation to many quarters of that vast country. In Grand Rapids, the best known and longest surviving of all the centres, there was a close community of Dutch Reform Protestants, who constituted an industrious and stable population. The furniture-making in Chicago was supported largely by the high percentage of German immigrants.

The strongest stylistic influence on American furniture in the mid-19th century was undoubtedly European, in particular British and French examples from the preceding century. Chippendale, Adam, Sheraton and Hepplewhite designs were available in the numerous antique shops which opened at that time and these were copied over and over again by American craftsmen, sometimes meticulously but usually with a high level of free interpretation and adaptation for a mass market. As mechanization began to supplant handwork, and more and more people were influenced by the idea of 'taste', furniture-makers applied additional surface decoration to their products in loose imitation of European models. They exaggerated the size of the furniture, the depth of the upholstery and the amount of the ornamentation, as a means of emphasizing the ideas of luxury and comfort so eagerly sought by the American consumers.

The degree to which the public wanted, and the manufacturers were supplying, 'taste', rather than simply functional furniture, for the new homes was quite explicit. The phenomenon was not limited to the urban areas but, with the assistance of mail order catalogues and efficient rail transportation, could reach the smallest town with few difficulties. The mass production industry focused in the Mid-West could supply the whole of America very quickly with all the goods it needed to consolidate its newly acquired standard of living.

Among the numerous furniture items to dominate the early period of American mass production was the heavy horse-hair sofa which came to epitomize the popular furniture aesthetic of the mid to late century. 19th-century American upholstery owed much to the way the British Victorian chair-makers had stuffed their chairs and sofas in order to achieve the exaggerated bulbous forms which expressed the newly acquired comfort and opulence of the 'nouveau riche' market. This was emulated in the USA for exactly the same social reasons, made possible by the development of new machines for making coiled wire springs and speeding up the stuffing process.

The mass production of upholstered furniture is well described by Sharon Darling in her book *Chicago Furniture*, in which she points out that, by the 1880s, *"Over half the output of furniture consisted of upholstered parlour furniture in that city"*, and that most firms were either specialized frame-makers or upholsterers, although a few, like S. Karpen and Bros, for instance, did provide the whole product. The largest frame-making concern belonged to the Austrian cabinet-maker Joseph Zangerle while the Karpen company was, in 1889, among the first to instal A. Freschl's Novelty Tufting Machine which was used to *"complete the backs and seats of less expensive couches"*. Chicago was ideally suited to supply the subsidiary materials used in upholstered furniture, such as hair and feathers, as it was the centre for the meat-packing industry. Metalworkers in that city also developed numerous versions of the wire springs essential for the upholstery process.

In his book *Mechanization Takes Command*, in which he outlines the difference between what he called 'ruling taste' and 'constituent furniture' – the latter being much less self-conscious and more directly functional – Sigfried Giedion went to great lengths to attack upholstered furniture as the curse of the 19th century, blaming it for what he considered to be its debased aesthetic standards and the demise of craftsmanship. *"The work of the upholsterer and the taste of the rising class seem to be marked out for one another"*, he contended.

In sharp contrast, one area of American furniture from the second

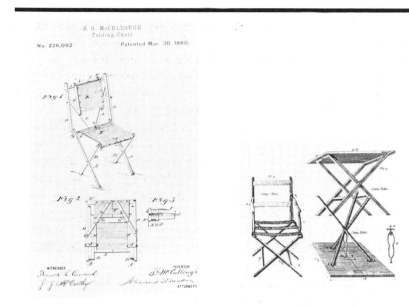

A patent drawing and model of a folding chair made from wood and canvas: Samuel G. McCullough patented his invention for the hinges and braces of this chair in 1880.

half of the 19th century met Giedon's approval, because it adhered to the criteria he applied to 'constituent' furniture. This was the patent furniture which grew directly out of combining the functions of, for instance, a sofa and bed in a single item for small accommodation and providing the necessary portability for a society which was increasingly on the move. Such functional requirements were not, however, the only stimuli behind the rash of new furniture inventions that came out of America at this time. Many were born of the demand for novelty on the part of the new consumers who sought desperately to

have something slightly different from their neighbours. The patent system was applied to furniture at this time to protect the inventors and manufacturers and to give them exclusive rights. The most distinctive inventions of the day were multipurpose items such as combined chairs and step ladders, and folding, reclining and rocking chairs of different sorts. Innovative though these products were, they only succeeded in touching the edge of the mass market which was preoccupied with enhancing its social status, for which purpose upholstered furniture was the most effective.

In 1913 George Leland Hunter wrote that, *"Taste is the most intimate and definite expression of personality: Even more than by his friends is it possible to judge a man by what appeals to him artistically"*. This idea, expressed in his book *Home Furnishings* telling Americans how to decorate and furnish their homes in good taste, penetrated deeply into the psyche of the mass market from the 1870s onwards. To meet this need, there emerged a series of furniture fashions which had very widespread influences. The first popular furniture style to make its appearance was one influenced by the book written by the Englishman Charles Eastlake, *Hints on Household Taste*. The American version was published in 1872 and its effects were more widespread than they had been in its country of origin. It served to popularize the ideas of the Aesthetic Movement on a much greater scale that it had in Britain.

Through its new emphasis on visual simplicity, the Eastlake fashion challenged the overt materialism and opulence of the earlier century and encouraged a more 'aesthetic' approach towards the domestic interior. It moved hand in hand with the Queen Anne Revival in architecture which swept America in the 1870s and 1880s bringing with it the influence of the Orient, in particular of Japan and China, and the reproduction of much Jacobean furniture which was illustrated in Eastlake's book. Inevitably the idiom was interpreted freely by many mass manufacturers and it featured strongly at the 1876 Centennial Exhibition in Philadelphia. By the end of the century a number of alternative styles had come on to the market place and they remained the main options available right up until the First World War. The Eastlake style had lost much of its popularity by this time and it was replaced by a number of new mass-produced styles each of which appealed to a slightly different market. American taste was gradually becoming more pluralistic.

By the first decade of the century cheap furniture was available in regular furniture stores and in the new large department stores, modelled on the European examples, such as Marshall Fields in Chicago. Furniture was still often bought in second hand

An illustration from an American home furnishings manual of 1913 showing four cheap chairs available on the market at that time – i.e. a 'Washington' chair (top left); a Chippendale-style oak chair (top right); a Windsor chair (bottom left); and a chair of the 'Mission' type (bottom right).

shops or it could be ordered directly either from firm's catalogues or by mail-order. S. Karpen and Bros, in Chicago for instance, became, in 1900, the first upholstered furniture company to sell directly, and it developed a policy of advertising to help it in its task. American furniture manufacturers worked closely with advertising agencies from the early days and were well ahead of the Europeans in this practice.

Whichever retail outlet they used, the American consumers had more or less the same range of options available to them from each source. It included some highly decorated furniture called 'golden oak' by the trade; Mission or Craftsman furniture items modelled on the pieces designed and made by Gustave Stickley, many of them cheap versions produced by Grand Rapids companies; some simple painted furniture which came into vogue in the 1890s; wicker or willow furniture pieces which came out of the garden and into the living-room in this period; and, last but not least, Thonet's bentwood furniture which was a little more expensive than its American counterparts but found its way, nonetheless, into numerous homes at this time as well as into restaurants and hotels.

Although these new styles of furniture were all on the market, reproduction period furniture remained highly fashionable and it too was available both in ready-made and custom-made versions. Opinions varied enormously about the 'tastefulness' or otherwise of the new furniture styles. George Leland Hunter, writing in support of furniture that was 'both beautiful and useful' was critical of much of the inexpensive furniture available in America at that time. He called the 'dwarfed and skimpy copies of Chippendale and Louis XV chairs', 'ridiculous', and condemned most Mission furniture for being 'cumbersome' and having 'an aptitude for falling apart'. Thonet bentwood furniture was praised however and described as being 'designed along the lines best adapted for machine production'. Hunter also commented that America had attained the same level as the English where mass production furniture was concerned. He mentioned High Wycombe as an interesting place to visit but remarked that it used 'machinery less and men more than on the American side of the Atlantic'.

Other popular furniture items of this period (designed with the small houses of the mass of the population in mind) included metal beds – some in brass but others plated in silver – which had spread from the hospital and prison into the home, and cheap wooden beds which copied the style of their metal counterparts. The fashion for wicker furniture, which was an offshoot of the vogue for all things Japanese, took a very strong hold in the first decade of the 20th century. While the wicker, rattan, reed and cane used was of Oriental origin, American prairie grass was also used. Bamboo, another Oriental material, was a source for furniture at this time, and was so cheap that a whole room of a New York apartment could be furnished with it for 25 dollars.

By the First World War, not only was a huge range of furniture styles available at a lower price than ever before for the American market, there was also a sense in which 'good taste' could be very easily purchased by the ordinary working consumer. Magazines, like the *Ladies Home Journal* and countless books published in these years, laid down the guidelines of a 'tasteful' home and the furniture industry made things available at a price most people could afford. While Europe still provided the main model for stylistic emulation, America was also aware of the need for an indigenous furniture aesthetic appropriate both to its technology and to its needs. With the examples of Shaker furniture, patent furniture and, to a certain extent, Mission furniture, to act as inspirations, America began to depend less on Europe as the style-leader. It was to be some decades, however, before the situation was reversed and the USA was showing Europe how to combine advanced technology with modern furniture design.

PART TWO

FURNITURE FOR THE MACHINE AGE (1915-1939)

THE inter-war period was a very rich and complex one in the story of modern domestic furniture. It witnessed, in the industrialized world, the continued expansion of the demand for new furniture on the part of a new category of consumers, and the sustained search, on the part of the manufacturer, for ways of making more furniture more cheaply.

Linked to these two factors, which grew inevitably out of pre-war developments, was another area of concern which had only been broached tentatively before 1914 by a number of brave pioneers. This was the increasingly burning question of what modern, mass-produced, mass-market furniture should look like.

The 19th century had witnessed a fight for supremacy among various styles revived from the past. The desperate need for social respectability, felt by many new consumers in those unstable years, had encouraged them to plump in the end for safety and conservatism. They opted for period styles in direct emulation of the wealthier sectors of society which had long ago established their canons of 'good taste'. Thus Queen Anne had succeeded Gothic and so on, so that by the turn of the century a range of alternative period styles was available to cater for the essential conservatism that has existed at some levels of the furniture market throughout the 20th century. The advent of machinery, which made more furniture pieces available to a larger proportion of the population, only served to widen the appeal of stylistic revivalism. In the early century many machines merely imitated and facilitated handwork, and made no stylistic changes to the furniture items they produced.

There was now a growing sense, however, that it was inappropriate to use modern machines merely to perpetuate old styles. This view was put forward, in particular, by a number of design promotion bodies, established in the early century to help their respective nations play a role within international trade, and it was demonstrated by the ideas of a handful of forward-thinking designers — mostly from the architectural sector. As a result of these attitudes a new furniture movement emerged which discouraged period styles and suggested instead, that a more appropriate furniture style should be formulated which would exploit the symbolic, as well as the practical, contribution of the machine to modern life.

These reforming ideals were not enough to persuade the mass of the population to start purchasing the simple undecorated furniture that grew out of this movement, and it would therefore be utterly false to suggest that 'modern' suddenly took over from 'period' as the furniture style of the inter-war years. It would be fair, however, to suggest that a combination of pioneering designs and the use of new materials (such as new metals and processed woods) led at this time to a stronger rejection of period styles than ever before.

The main argument for a modern aesthetic came from an international group of avant-garde architects and designers who were active in this period and who are usually seen as the major protagonists of the Modern Movement in furniture, Among them were Le Corbusier, Mies van der Rohe, Gerrit Rietveld, Mart Stam, Marcel Breuer and Frank Lloyd Wright. There were, of course, many other factors to consider as well – social, economic and technological. One important development was the fact that the many new homes of this period, whether houses or flats, all tended to be considerably smaller than the average Victorian home. Also the growing demand for cheaper production led to the use of standardized and interchangeable compo-

nents, and to rational 'flow' production within the factory. These factors tended to discourage variations in style. Finally the new materials and the new ways of working traditional ones, tended to encourage simple, flush surfaces and basic, undecorated forms. All these factors have to be considered together in any discussion of the emergence of the 'modern' furniture style.

These modernizing tendencies did not of course dictate the way in which all furniture developed. They existed alongside deep-seated views about the psychological and social need for comfort, luxury, status and security – all of them essential functions for furniture. Gradually, however, 'modern' took on a rationale of its own and, by the beginning of the Second World War, the international picture of mass-produced furniture looked very different from how it had seemed in the tattered aftermath of the First World War.

Marcel Breuer's cantilevered dining chairs in tubular steel, with seats and backs in black lacquered wood and cane. Designed at the Bauhaus in 1928 the 'Cesca' chair has through numerous reworkings, come to represent the ideals of the Modern movement for a mass audience.

4

STANDARDS IN EUROPEAN FURNITURE

PROGRESSIVE ideas about the appearance of furniture for the modern age came mainly from Continental Europe in the inter-war years. It was their models which influenced later developments in Britain and the USA. In Holland, for instance, the De Stijl architect-designer, Gerrit Rietveld, first developed a chair along geometric, machine-age principles, using block board and machine planed wood. In Germany, Marcel Breuer and Mies van der Rohe experimented with a material only previously used in bicycle frame manufacture – tubular steel. In Finland, Alvar Aalto produced his modern vision of a chair constructed from plywood.

These men, along with many others, had something in common which enabled them to take such radical steps forward. They were all experienced in architecture and tended, as a result, to see furniture in the light of the joint concerns of con-

Gerrit Rietveld's Red/Blue chair of 1918. Made from machine-processed wood, this chair was among the first to exploit the strict rectilinear forms of the machine aesthetic which characterized much new architecture in this period.

struction and spatial configuration – themes which had been dominant among progressive architects since the 1890s. For them, the chair became a sculptural 'sitting object'. This was in direct contrast with the idea of the chair as a provider of maximum comfort for the human body (which inspired the 19th-century heavily upholstered chair), or the idea of the chair as a status object (which had led to exaggerated decoration).

These avant-garde ideas, which were rooted in the construction of simple elements and the use of modern materials and techniques, rejected historical styles, and proposed, instead, a modern aesthetic which related directly to the context of the 20th century.

Many writers about modern furniture imply that these highly innovative designs set the pace for the rest of the century, but this overlooks the fact that these designs were responding to the same forces that affected all furniture. In addition, most people were introduced to simple modern shapes, not through contact with a few esoteric examples, but through the numerous magazine articles and guides to furnishing and interior decoration which pleaded with them to move away from period furniture. The effects were not felt overnight, however, and it was to be some time before it was possible to talk about 'modern' as a mass furniture style.

One of the motivating forces behind the modern furniture movement was the wish, on the part of a number of European governments and official bodies, to democratize furniture. They wanted to provide furnishings for the many new working class housing and apartments which were being built at this time. A housing plan for Vienna in the early 1920s had included 60,000 working men's apartments, for which Josef Hoffmann had been brought in to design several large-area, low cost chairs. The Viennese experiment encouraged Germany to follow suit and Frankfurt, for instance, developed a highly systematic programme in the 1920s to meet its housing needs. It depended totally upon the concepts of rationalization and standardization to provide fittings and furnishings for the new housing. A set of 'Frankfurt Standards' was created for the task, and a number of designers, including Ferdinand Kramer and Mart Stam, set about working on a series of inexpensive and visually very simple furniture pieces for the new dwellings which were mass-produced by large German companies. Their work was heavily influenced by Christine Frederick's book *The New Housekeeping* based on American ideas about household management from the 1880s.

The Frankfurt experiment was in its turn highly influential in a number of other countries, including Sweden where the Social Democratic government of the 1930s instigated a series of projects with the same reforming attitude towards modern design. The spirit of American mass production underpinned many of the new ideas that grew up in Germany in this period and, by the 1920s, modular systems had been absorbed into furniture production on a significant scale. By the 1920s, also, the German furniture industry as a whole had become a major force on the world market. While it catered largely for the trade in reproduction furniture, there was also a strong interest in simple, standardized pieces made of new and modified materials.

Wood remained, however, the dominant material for cheap modern furniture in this period. The work of the Deutsche Werkstätten in Hellerau continued into the 1920s, when Adolf Schneck's designs characterized its

A writing desk designed by Adolf Schneck, made from standardized parts. It was one element in a series of furniture items designed for mass production by the Deutscher Werkstätten in Hellerau in 1923.

forays into modern wooden furniture. Schneck established a furniture research section at the Stuttgart School for Applied Arts where he developed composite wood boards (plywood or blockboard as they came to be called), and new methods of veneering and jointing these materials together. In describing their influence on modern furniture, Tim Benton has written that, *"The 'modern look' in furniture is the result of achieving undifferentiated surfaces and clean block-like forms from the assembly of wide boards veneered right across with no mouldings. The origins of everything that we recognize in wooden furniture from the late 1930s stems from these changes".* This claim has much truth in it. The move from decorated, carved and inlaid to plain wooden surfaces was a radical one which paved the way for the future, and the simple wooden dining-chairs that Schneck designed for the Schwarz brothers in 1928, as well as his designs for bookcases and cabinets, had a standardized, anonymous quality which makes them hard to date. Erich Dieckmann, a member of the Bauhaus School in Dessau, also worked on a number of 'standard' wooden furniture pieces for production, as did a number of other notable designers in this period. Many of them, including Kramer, Schneck and the Austrian Josef Frank, executed designs for the Thonet company (which made an economic come-back in the 1920s) which fit into this category. Many leading architects of the day were fascinated by the simple, machine-made products of the Thonet company. Le Corbusier, in France, went as far as to incorporate them into a number of his interiors, along with the 'built-in' furniture items that he designed himself.

Standard furniture in the new material, tubular steel, was more expensive that its wooden equivalents but, by the end of the 1920s had

Guiseppe Terragni's cantilevered side chair designed for the Fascist Party headquarters in Como in 1936. It was one of the first examples of tubular steel furniture to appear on Italian soil.

begun to be taken seriously as a commercial proposition, although it was not as yet really aimed at the domestic market. The first company to sell polished steel furniture made from extruded tube was owned by Marcel Breuer (who first invented this kind of furniture) and his partner Kalman Lengyel, and was called Standard Möbel. They established the company in order to mass-produce Breuer's designs from the Bauhaus, but were thwarted in their efforts to do so. The Thonet company was, however, very quick to see the potential of the material and in late 1928,

bought the rights to a number of Breuer's designs. These they mass-produced in the same way as they had their bent-wood pieces, i.e. from a minimum number of parts which could be simply screwed together. Their products were available with either a nickel- or chromium-plated finish. The main advantage of steel chairs over wooden ones was their durability and, as far as the modern architects were concerned, their aesthetic. The chairs conformed very well to the simple, rational anonymous style they sought so eagerly.

The story of tubular steel furniture in the 1930s demonstrates the degree to which the Modern style was, or was not, accepted by the majority of people. Its varied receptions in France, Britain, the USA, Italy and Scandinavia reflected the varying attitudes of conservatism and innovation within those countries towards domestic furnishing. In Germany, in the 1930s, it was outlawed, along with the Bauhaus, whereas in Italy it provided exactly the right image for Guiseppe Terragni's interior of his Casa del Fasci in Como. The two fascist regimes clearly had a very different approach towards the Modern Movement. A number of the avant-garde Italian Rationalist architects, in fact, including Pagano, Levi Montalcini and Mucchi, experimented with tubular steel furniture seeing it as the perfect expression of the modern age.

In the USA the abundance of ready steel made it a popular and fairly cheap material for furniture, and tubular steel items came out of the American factories in large numbers from the mid 1930s onwards. In Britain the PEL company took on the production of tubular steel furniture, but its uses were restricted to the contract market and interiors of the few fringe examples of Modern Movement buildings which appeared in the 1930s. On the whole the British public rejected its harshness and coldness, preferring the warmth and essential humanism of wood.

Although the French examples of tubular steel furniture, designed by such leading avant-garde architects of the day as Le Corbusier and Eileen Gray, have remained classics of modern design, they were more exclusive both in their aesthetic and in their production runs than their German equivalents and had, therefore, very little mass impact in the 1920s and 1930s. It was only later with the revival and reproduction of these designs in the 1960s and 1970s that they became widely known. For the most part French furniture remained an élitist phenomenon until considerably later on. The Art Deco movement was, in its early French manifestations, merely an extension of the same cabinet-making business that had underpinned the Art Nouveau movement and caused its downfall.

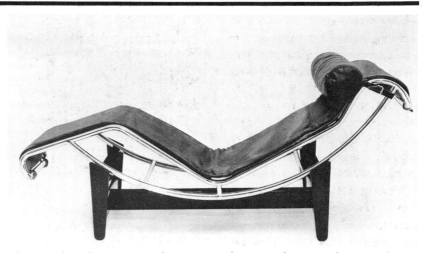

The French architect, Le Corbusier's two furniture designs – the 'Grand Confort' armchair and the chaise longue – were designed in 1928 and used tubular steel for their basic structure.

As a modern style, however, it had a mass impact in a number of other countries, in particular in the USA and, to a certain extent in Britain (although here it was more visible in public environments than in the home). In France, it remained an exclusive affair indulged in only by the very wealthy. Furniture designed by men like Emile Ruhlmann, and interior decoration by teams like Suë et Mare, were commissioned privately by affluent clients but they failed to influence the homes of ordinary people.

German furniture from the 1920s was of greater significance to the world of mass production. German industry at this time was supported by the Werkbund, whose brief was to

Below: A four-piece folding screen designed by Eileen Gray in 1930 which consisted of a wooden frame with perforated steel and finished in either red, black, grey or ivory lacquer.

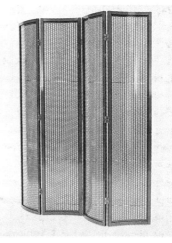

evolve simple, modern design which could be mass-produced and available to everybody. The furniture it produced laid the foundations for much that was to emerge later. Tim Benton explains that a suburban dweller's furnishings in a Nazi exhibition of 1937 looked exactly like the ones supported by the Werkbund in the early 1920s and that the German Werkstätten in Hellerau continued, through the 1930s, to produce simple modern industrial furniture in both plywood and steel. It was this furniture, rather than the avant-garde Bauhaus projects, that was to have a lasting effect on the way the Modern style evolved in Germany later in the century.

Unlike those in Britain, Scandinavia's craft traditions had not been eroded by rapid and large-scale industrialization. Instead, industry came both late and slowly to those Nordic countries, with the result that it was still possible to talk of craft traditions there at the beginning of this century. It was also at this time that Sweden, Denmark and Finland were beginning to become aware of their new-found independence, and their experiments in craft and design reflected their search for national style. They combined indigenous folk traditions with echoes of certain international styles – in particular Art Nouveau. Each of the Scandinavian countries developed a range of objects, including furniture pieces in birch and pine, which were based on the simple forms of their vernacular craft styles.

Wood remained pre-eminent within Scandinavian furniture in the 20th century and formed its main contribution to the modern style. The countries in question were all poor in raw materials, but they had no shortage of wood, in particular birch and pine in Sweden and Finland, and beech in Denmark. Simple wooden benches, chairs, tables, beds, wardrobes and cupboards, with the addition of a simple woven rug on the floor, had been typical of the traditional Scandinavian dwelling place for many centuries and the austerity and simplicity of this interior style helped form the ethic which was to underpin all modern Scandinavian thinking about furniture and interior design. It embraced tradition, craft skills, and natural materials, but it also stood for a highly refined, democratic belief that simple products should be made available to everybody, and that craftsmanship need not necessarily be exclusive. This humanistic philosophy behind Scandinavian design depended upon their having a highly homogeneous society with little extreme poverty or wealth, and a history without either a sudden break between craft and industry, or a mass migration from the country to the town.

It was in Sweden that these ideals were first articulated and where a Scandinavian furniture movement began to emerge after the First World War. The turn of the century had witnessed an emphasis on the light, simple Swedish interior typified by the nostalgic drawings of Carl Larssen and the traditional pine furniture of Carl Westman, both of which were suffused by a delicacy and a simplicity which owed everything to Swedish folk interiors. These ideals, summarized by Ellen Key in her book *Beauty for All*, formed the basis of a design philosophy best elucidated by the architect Gregor Paulsson in his book of 1919 entitled, in the same spirit, *More Beautiful Everyday Things*. Furniture played a vital role within the Swedish design movement, which focused on the home and, in particular, the domestic interior. In the years following the First World War numerous efforts were made to evolve simple, wooden furniture which would provide the basic equipment for the working man's home. In 1917 an exhibition was held in Lillevachs, entitled *The Home*, consisting of a number of simply and traditionally furnished interiors. The architects Gunnar Asplund and Carl Malmsten, later to become highly influential figures within the modern Swedish furniture movement, developed ranges of cabinet-made wooden furniture which fulfilled, aes-

Above: Mies van der Rohe's cantilevered chrome-plated tubular steel chairs of 1931. Available with either leather or cane seats, and with or without arms, this design quickly became an icon of modern design and has been produced throughout this century first by Thonet and later by Knoll International.

thetically at least, this democratic brief. Their designs were essentially modified versions of traditional pieces, using wood and cane and incorporating traditional motifs and structures. Asplund exhibited a combined kitchen/living room, a very early example of this particular solution to the problem of reduced living spaces.

In Scandinavia the idea of simplicity in furniture was linked exclusively, in this period, with craft rather than machine production. The Scandinavian furniture industry, meanwhile, was pre-occupied, as in so many other countries, with reproduction and fancy pieces aimed at an upper middle class market.

The 1920s in Sweden marked an interlude in the forming of the ideological link between craft and democracy. (It was to be later resumed in the work of men like G.A. Berg, Bruno Mathsson and Josef Frank.) During that decade the Swedish architects and designers were seduced, first, by Neo-Classicism and later by the new metal, machine-aesthetic furniture that was emerging from Germany. The Stockholm Exhibition of 1930 was dominated by this type of furniture which seemed, temporarily, to have betrayed the more traditionalist ideals of the early century. The Swedish public, however, like the British, preferred the humanism, warmth and traditional associations of wood to the qualities of tubular steel and by the 1930s, the years of the Social Democratic Government in Sweden, the pendulum had swung back again to a more traditionalist approach to modern furniture.

The decreasing size of most living-spaces was also a major determining factor in the evolution of Swedish fur-

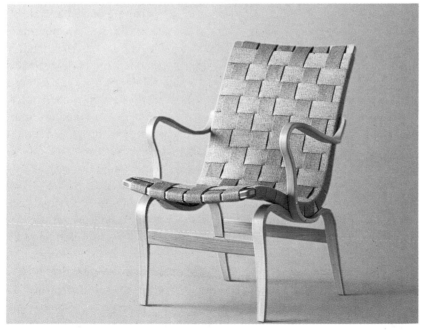

Bruno Mathsson's 'Pernilla' chair, with its laminated beech frame, was designed with a seat made of either leather or woven canvas. Although appearing first in 1939 it is still in production today and has become one of Sweden's classic modern chairs.

niture in the 1930s. Although the Swedish furniture industry was still essentially craft-based, machines were being introduced to perform a number of tasks. Among the most innovative designs from this period were those of Bruno Mathsson who, working with a small production unit on Värnamo, designed and manufactured variations of an easy chair made of bent laminated wood and covered with either canvas or leather webbing depending on the price. It has since become ubiquitous in Sweden, symbolizing the heroic period of modern Swedish furniture and combining the demands of tradition, modernity, comfort and lightness. The chair's curved forms are defined by the human shape and Mathsson spent much time measuring the human body and deciding upon the best position in which to mould the seating support. Comfort is provided by the actual form of the object and by the flexibility of the webbing rather than by heavy upholstery which denies seating objects a graceful silhouette.

The other major protagonist of what, by the end of the decade, had become known as 'Swedish Modern' (a movement which embraced the whole range of applied arts) was the Viennese architect Josef Frank, who arrived in Sweden in the early 1930s. He moved away at this time from the functionalism he had recently been expressing in his work for the Werkbund Siedlung, to a more humanistic decorative interior style which owed much to his Viennese roots. Working from 1934 onwards for the Svenskt Tenn shop in Stockholm, he designed ranges of mahogany cabinets on plinths inspired by 18th-century British examples, brightly coloured exotic textiles inspired by primitive cultures, brass lamps, graceful dining and side-chairs with tapered legs and steel and wicker furniture which was reserved for the garden. Through Svenskt Tenn, Frank's designs were aimed at a wealthy market, but many of their features fed directly into the Swedish style which was so influential internationally in the years after 1945. It was a style epitomizing values directly opposed to the more mechanistic model of the German avant-garde architects and designers. Frank proposed an eclectic, humanistic aesthetic in which man, rather than the machine, was the symbolic centre. A critic at the New York World's Fair of 1939, at which Frank presented a widely admired interior described the Swedish aesthetic as 'a movement towards sanity in design', thus contrasting the moderation of Sweden's efforts with what he saw as the fanaticism of several other countries' contributions.

If Sweden's offering to modern furniture design in this period was one of 'sanity', Denmark's was

The Austrian architect-designer Josef Frank designed this cabinet for the Swedish shop, Svenskt Tenn, in the mid 1940s.

the equally important one of anthropometrics – in other words measuring furniture to fit the human being. The emphasis here was less psychological than physical, and the work done in Denmark at this time was to have a tremendous influence on international furniture in the post-war period. In many ways Denmark is better known than Sweden as the home of modern Scandinavian furniture. This is because of the strong modern furniture tradition in that country, which combined the pioneering work on anthropometrics of Kaare Klint with, from 1927 onwards, the contribution of the

Danish Cabinet-Makers Guild in sponsoring modern design. As in Sweden, mass-production industry was late in developing in Denmark and, when it did so, it devoted itself to reproduction rather than modern pieces.

Kaare Klint's role within modern Danish furniture was of major importance not only in establishing the need for precise furniture measurements, but also in reviving traditional chair-types, and in teaching the new generation of pioneering furniture-craftsmen. A Neo-Classicist in his early years, Klint had, by 1917, already initiated his studies of measurement and proportion. In the 1920s, with his students at the Academy of Fine Art in Copenhagen, he set up a programme of systematic measurement studies of 18th-century English Chippendale pieces. His famous light beech chair, designed for Gruntvig's Church, was based on a Mediterranean model, but also owed much to his measurement studies. Storage units too came under his systematic scrutiny, and a cupboard for tableware which he designed in 1926 was the result of very careful measuring of the pieces that had to be stored in it.

When, in the years after the Second World War, small living spaces increased the need for rationalized storage systems, the influence of Klint's pioneering work was much in evidence. When certain traditional furniture-types were revived, Klint's reworking of the deckchair in 1933 provided an important example, as did his 'Safari' chair of the same year. Klint remained committed to cabinet-making throughout his career and worked, for many years, in close association with the same craftsman, Rudolf Rasmussen.

The importance of cabinet-making to modern Danish furniture cannot be over-estimated. From the late 1920s onwards the combined efforts of the designer-craftsmen provided the impetus for the new furniture aesthetic which, however exclusive in manufacture, was founded upon a firm democratic belief. Denmark was a country with a relatively small, wealthy population and an unbroken craft tradition, and it was therefore easy for craftsmen to play a major role in its modern furniture movement. In the late 1920s, the cabinet-makers guild initiated an annual exhibition, as a direct response to the products of the newly developed furniture industry and to the recent surge in foreign imports. The craftsmen also realized that to survive they would have to co-operate with designers and so the concept of the designer-craftsman became an early reality in Denmark. Determined to stem the tide of the sudden influx of period and 'inferior' furniture, the cabinet-makers set out to show that they could provide the formula that would satisfy both the aesthetic and the social requirements of a Danish modern furniture movement. While the industry wooed the middle classes the cabinet-makers, somewhat ironically, emphasized, for instance in an exhibition in 1930, furniture for a two-roomed flat, showing that their brief was essentially a democratic one. It was an emphasis which remained central to the Danish Modern project in the 1940s which, through the work of Klint's pupil, Borge Mogensen, demonstrated to the rest of the world the democratic commitment of the Danish cabinet-maker. Before the Second World War neither Swedish nor Danish furniture had penetrated an international market. After 1945, however, they dominated the international scene for almost two decades.

The third important Scandinavian country in this context, Finland, realized the importance of expanding its markets internationally at an earlier stage. Finland exported the work of its major furniture-architect, Alvar Aalto, to both Britain and the USA in the 1930s, thereby establishing internationally what came to be known as the 'blond look', due to Aalto's use of birchwood.

The story of modern Finnish furniture begins at the turn of the century and stands independently of events in both Sweden and Denmark.

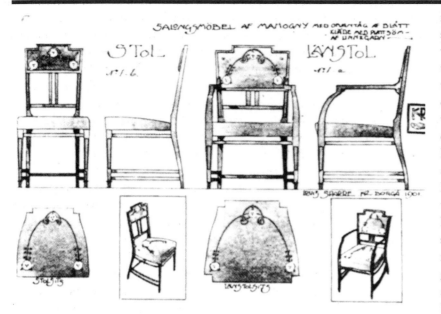

Mahogany dining room chairs designed by Louis Sparre in 1901 in a style which came to represent the Finnish version of Judendstil.

The short burst of progressive activity in the years around 1900 was due in part to the British Arts and Crafts Movement and the Northern European 'Jugendstil', both of which had a strong influence on Finnish architects and craftsmen like Eliel Saarinen and the Swede, Louis Sparre, who came to Finland in 1889 and founded the Iris industrial arts factory in Porvoo. The movement did not represent (as it did in Britain) a rejection of industrialization, yet to affect Finland in a major way, but it indicated simply an upsurge of national feeling.

Although Finland was late to industrialize, its wood industry was among the first to be developed and in the 1870s mills began to spring up. Gradually the Finnish furniture industry grew large enough to take advantage of it. The years of expansion were between 1908 and 1918 as a result of exports to Russia. In 1908, for instance, there were only 35 carpenter's workshops in Finland but by 1918 this had risen to 175. In 1910, to cite another example, a company called the Boman Furniture Factory had 600 employees. Its manufacturing techniques were, however, craft-based and it wasn't until 1918 when a man called Aukusti Avonius, the son of a joiner, transformed the company

into the Lahti Carpenter Factory that standardized furniture production was introduced into Finland. Even then it was the exception rather than the rule. This company survived the effects of the Russian revolution which killed off many other firms and expanded in the 1930s when it fulfilled the consumer demands of Finland and provided furniture for the new houses being built. The main styles of the day were period revivals, particularly those of the baroque and rococo styles. In 1931 the company changed its name to Asko and initiated a programme of bringing in interior architects to design furniture for it but without much popular success. Although limited to production in birch, their work tended to reflect the modern style found elsewhere in Europe at that time.

Finland's greatest contribution to international modern furniture in this period lay in the work of the architect Alvar Aalto. He stands out as an isolated figure working on what he called 'architectural accessories' intended for industrial manufacture. From the beginning he had a shrewd awareness of the international market that lay beyond Finland. Like Mathsson's furniture which followed them, Aalto's pieces appealed to a middle class intellectual market in those countries which were wary of the German-produced tubular steel. His furniture comfortably combined

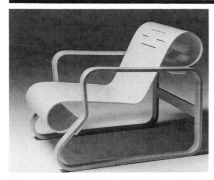

Alvar Aalto's 'Chair 41' designed between 1930 and 1933 for his Paimio Sanitorium.

new technological processes and new, light, modern forms with traditional materials, thereby providing the perfect formula for those who preferred humanistic to mechanistic modern furniture.

Aalto's first chairs grew out of experiments with bent plywood and laminated wood which he carried out while developing furniture for his Paimio Sanitorium between 1929 and 1933. His aim was to make wood elastic and, to this end, he developed a chair which had a unified plywood seat and back curved in two dimensions to match the shape of the body, with arms of laminated birch wood glued on to the sides. He was, in essence, interpreting the principles of tubular steel furniture in wood and thereby producing pieces which blended as easily into a private home as they did into a public space or institution. Like his Danish counter-

parts, Aalto was also interested in the problem of the decreasing size of living-spaces and in 1930 he was the prime mover in an exhibition entitled 'Rationalization of the Home'. It was for his display there that he developed a small stacking stool which, again exploiting bent wood, made the maximum use of minimum space. Like the chairs, the stools were manufactured in series by a small family business in Turku.

The other technological innovation pioneered by Aalto in these years was a method of joining wood to wood allowing for an organic unison of the vertical with the horizontal plane. Later in the 1930s this was developed into a more sophisticated 'Y' joint which permitted the intersection of three dimensions. These innovations helped increase the visual

Alvar Aalto's bentwood tea trolley was designed in 1936 and retailed through Artek.

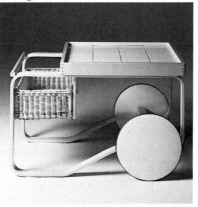

unity of his pieces.

In 1935, with his wife Aino and the art critic Nils Gustav Hahl, Aalto opened a shop in Helsinki called 'Artek' as a means of marketing his architectural accessories which by now included textiles and glass as well as furniture. In 1933 Britain's *Architectural Review* organized an exhibiton which made Aalto's products visible in that country and in the same year it received much attention at the Triennale in Milan. In 1939 New York played host to it at the New York World's Fair of that year, and, in many ways, Aalto's work had a greater impact abroad than at home.

By 1939 the concept of 'Scandinavian Modern' had become consolidated internationally as a furniture and interior style. It suited the searchers after 'good modern design' as well as providing reassurance to the ordinary consumer. It was a gentle, human style which contained a high level of democratic idealism and which was also modern and technologically advanced. Its elegant simplicity could be reproduced either by hand or by machine. On a number of levels, therefore, Scandinavian Modern was the first mass furniture style which had any real international presence and, by the late 1940s, it had succeeded in suggesting, for a time at least, that the days of period and reproduction furniture were, if not over, at least limited.

5

FROM PERIOD TO MODERN STYLE IN THE USA

IN the first three decades of this century, America also had its share of architect-designed furniture which embraced the high-minded principles of the European Modern Movement. Most notable were pieces by Frank Lloyd Wright, Richard Neutra, Rudolf Schindler, and Josef Urban. While some of these pioneering Moderns were natives of the USA many were emigrés from Germany or Austria who brought with them ideas acquired in the 'Old World'.

In the 1920s America was considered, by the European companies who exported furniture to the 'New World', to be an exceptionally conservative market. Period style still dominated the choice of most consumers who saw it as bringing them 'taste', history and respectability. The Thonet company produced special furniture lines just for the USA, most of which had a period feel to them. The introduction to its American catalogue described this emphasis:

"Thonet Brothers inc, have been able to meet the discriminating taste of the most exciting architect or decorator in reproducing the finest examples of period furniture of the old Spanish, French and English craftsmanship without sacrificing the prime essentials of bentwood". Thus, while the USA was, mechanically and industrially speaking, more advanced than anywhere else (except perhaps Germany), its taste preferences showed little evidence of a new aesthetic for the machine-dominated modern age.

This could largely be explained by the existence of huge numbers of middle class consumers — many of who had come from Europe and were loathe to leave the security of the past totally behind them — as well as by the quantity of furniture manufacturers based in Grand Rapids and Chicago who were able to provide mass-produced, reproduction pieces at relatively low prices. Although the avant-garde architects — Wright, Schindler, Neutra and the others — were busy experimenting with such progressive ideas as 'built-in' and modular furniture for private clients, it was to be some time before the American population was to be convinced that modern furniture was an acceptable alternative to reproduction pieces. By the end of the 1930s there were signs, however, that smaller living spaces and the economic need to use new materials (predominantly plywood, blockboard and tubular steel) were encouraging a lighter, simpler taste in furniture. A number of industrial designers, among them Gilbert Rhode and Russel Wright, began working with mass production companies in the 1930s to ensure that 'well-designed', cheap, modern furniture could be made available to whoever wanted it.

The inter-war years in the USA saw the boom period of the 1920s followed by a slump, in the wake of the Wall Street Crash of 1929. The effects

The interior of Richard Schindler's Lovell house from the 1920s showing that architect's dramatic use of open space and minimal furnishing.

of this were felt as strongly by the furniture trade as by other manufacturing industries. Also, around 1920, the lumber in Michigan, which had supplied Grand Rapids, began to run out. Three of Grand Rapids' biggest firms – Luce, Sligh and Berkey and Gay – went under in the depression and, as a reaction to the pressures put upon them, a number of the Mid West furniture companies began to concentrate on quality rather than quantity as a means of preserving their markets. This was exemplified by the decision of the Baker Furniture Company, under the leadership of the founder's son Hollis Baker. It started to manufacture furniture which, he

maintained, he would buy to furnish his own home, rather than the cheap reproduction pieces that the company had depended upon until then. This involved thinking much more carefully about the designs of the furniture, whether reproduction or modern. The southern firms now began to grow and indeed to take over where Grand Rapids left off, supplying the lower income groups with the furniture they wanted. This process was, however, a very gradual one and only became fully apparent by the late 1930s.

Design, in these years of tough competition, was an increasingly important consideration both for the

furniture companies and for the consumers with their smaller incomes who became increasingly style-conscious. They were encouraged in this direction by a number of 'tastemakers' who set out in this period to help the new consumers to discriminate between 'good' and 'bad' design. Many new dwellings were built in the inter-war years to house the expanding urban and suburban populations, including villas and apartments, and there was general concern that the decisions about decorating and furnishing them should encourage the best in American manufacturing.

In 1932 the Presidents Conference on Home Building and Home Ownership was held in Washington. The Committee on Home Furnishings and Decoration stressed the need to bring *"beauty as well as convenience, comfort and appropriateness of furnishing within the reach of families of quite moderate means"*. It considered the majority of furniture available in department stores and furniture houses (which was aimed at people with medium and low incomes) to be both ugly and inappropriate. The Committee's task was to provide every homemaker with information which would help him or her make 'wiser' decisions, in the hopes that this would encourage the manufacturers to do better. To this end, it set about an analysis of the present situation in terms of markets, incomes and

A dining chair designed in the Arts and Crafts tradition by the American architect-designer Frank Lloyd Wright in 1904.

tion received under 15,000 dollars a year, and these fell into the lowest income group. For them it recommended the need for *"low-priced furniture, which should be good in design and as good in respect to construction and materials as the price will allow"*. It concluded that the most dangerous thing of all was the tendency towards *"false style stimulation"* which suggested that *"taste is the whim of the moment"*.

In the 1930s, the move towards the *"absolute simplicity of thought and outline"*, recommended by the Committee, gradually emerged, thanks to the increased use of new

materials and the work of a few designers and manufacturers who took the project on board.

In the early 1930s, however, fashionable taste at the top end of the market was provided by craftsmen and interior decorators. The furniture which fulfilled the needs of this particular market relied heavily on the highly voguish and expensive Art Deco style imported from France. Luxurious materials were combined with the stepped forms that were being used in the new skyscrapers and designers such as Paul Frankl and Donald Deskey, together with many others who had recently arrived from

budgets in order to ascertain exactly what was required.

The growing use of the specialist-decorator (predominantly a French influence) was commented upon in the report presented by the Committee, as was his role in helping raise the taste standards of the upper classes. Inevitably, however, people with medium or small incomes could not afford his services but depended upon stores to provide them with information. Quality furnishing was seen as relating directly to income, and the report stated that most of the popula-

Bedroom furniture by Gilbert Rhode designed for the Herman Miller Company and displayed at the 'Century of Progress' exhibition held in Chicago in 1933/4.

Germany and Vienna, set about providing the American rich with a style to suit its opulence. Cheaper versions of this luxury style quickly penetrated the mass market and, later in the decade, the style became associated increasingly with the showy, modernistic idiom referred to as 'borax'.

Interest in new materials remained fundamental to American manufacturing in the 1930s. At Chicago's Century of Progress exhibition of 1933, for example, (which was dominated by the work of the decorators, and masterminded by Josef Urban, another immigrant from Vienna) the new materials, among them rubber, flexwood, veneers, aluminium, glass, formica, cork and linoleum came into their own. All of them found their way into furniture in one form or another. Also in 1933, the public saw, for the first time, mass-produced furniture in tubular steel produced by the Howell company which was based in Geneva, Illinois. These pieces showed that new materials brought their own aesthetic with them, and the tubular-steel chair forms designed by Wolfgang Hoffman (son of the Viennese architect Josef Hoffmann), with their bent metal frames and lightly upholstered seats, had little in common with the decorated, faceted shapes of the French school. Hoffmann moved to Illinois after

1933 and designed exclusively for the Howell company between 1934 and 1942. His 'S' chairs from the mid-30s were produced and sold in high volume. Often they were used as 'dinette' sets in small kitchens and combination living-dining rooms. Tubular steel furniture was produced in bulk through the 1930s by numerous Chicago firms as well. The American public absorbed it quite naturally and it acquired, therefore, none of the exclusive associations that it had in Europe.

From 1933 onwards it became apparent to a number of manufacturing companies that cheapness didn't necessarily imply either inferior workmanship or total dependence upon period or European styles. A number of industrial designers arrived at the same conclusion at the same time, including Russel Wright, Gilbert Rhode, Donald Deskey and Kem Weber. A commentator in *Architectural Forum* of 1934 also noticed that *"The awkward angular fantastic objects with which the market was flooded during the early 'modernist' craze has given place to furniture which embodies grace as well as the maximum in scientifically*

A tubular-steel framed upholstered armchair designed by Wolfgang Hoffmann for the Howell Company in the mid 1930s. In the USA tubular-steel furniture was manufactured in vast numbers and became highly popular between the wars.

A prototype of the Chicago-based Howell Company's chromsteel serving cart designed by Wolfgang Hoffmann in 1935.

determined comfort." What he was observing was a switch from the obsession with France and Vienna as the main stylistic stimuli in furniture, to the new influence of simple 'blond' Scandinavian design.

Russel Wright was committed, however, to what he called 'modern American native design'. In 1933, he designed a set of furniture items and three-piece sectional sofas for a company called Heywood-Wakefield, which would, he claimed, introduce a sense of variety into the home. His best known and most popular range of furniture was produced later, in 1935, by the Conant-Ball company and marketed by Macy's under the name of 'American Modern'. It aimed to provide the widest possible sector of the public with functional modern furniture at the lowest possible price. As one way of keeping down costs he did away with veneers and made the furniture instead from pieces of solid maple, the wood of the American pioneers. The appeal of his furniture lay in its sturdy, straight-forward and craftsmanlike forms. Its construction was very basic, the pieces were simply overlapped or butted together and the upholstery was minimal. Its usefulness was enhanced by hidden storage areas and generous arm rests. Stylistically the pieces had a workmanlike quality and combined a sense of modern efficiency with tradition (expressed in the choice of material). Maple was in abundant supply in the USA at this time so it was perfectly economical to use solid planks of it. Later Wright introduced the 'blond' maple finish which became typical of so much mass-produced American furniture in the 1930s. In spite of the indigenous quality of Wright's furniture it also had many Scandinavian overtones so increasing its fashionable appeal in this period.

The decreasing size of urban apartments and of suburban and rural houses was a recurrent theme of the mid to late 1930s and gave rise to a number of experiments with cheap modern furniture, influenced primarily by work in Germany. Kem Weber, for instance, a German immigrant working on the West Coast of the USA designed, in 1931, a range of laminated wood furniture known as 'Bentlock' which could be knocked down for shipment, while Gilbert Rhode, a new arrival from Vienna, worked with similar practical concerns in mind.

One writer about 'good taste' in home decorating in 1936 distinguished between two styles of American modern furniture. One she called 'Classic Modern', which depended upon the occasional borrowing from period styles, and the other she called 'Functional' into which category she placed the work of Rhode for the Kroehler Manufacturing Company, a firm based in the Chicago area. This 'Functional' style was characterized by its formal simplicity, and its flat, smooth surfaces which, the writer claimed were influenced by the vogue for streamlining, 'now a commonplace in the design of trains and motor-cars'.

The other recurrent justification for the 'functional, modern' style was its hygienic quality (no nooks or crannies to conceal dirt) and the fact that it reduced dusting to a minimum. The same labour-saving rationale that had previously been applied to washing-machines and dish-washers was now seen as relevant to furniture as well. Aluminium, stainless steel and chrome were frequently praised for the fact that 'they retain their luster without the drudgery of polishing'. The labour-saving argument natur-

ally grew in importance as servants disappeared and more and more housewives went out to work. This social change had a major effect on the evolution of modern domestic furniture in the USA.

In the context of modern living, the simple comfort of home furniture was seen as providing restfulness in a hectic world of 'business, sports and social engagements'. Rhode's 'Living-Dining-Sleeping' range for one room consisted of a set of standard and largely interchangeable units comprising bookcases, cupboards, chairs, sofas, coffee-tables and a utility chest. Reduced incomes and smaller living quarters encouraged the 'unit' idea which had begun with steel cabinets

and cupboards for the kitchen. Rhode's furniture was also multipurpose. A gateleg table, for instance, came complete with three drawers and a cabinet in the pedestal support to store flatware, writing materials, table linens, the toaster or the coffee percolator, and its surface served alternatively as a console, a writing table or a dining table. Equally the cabinet in one of the bookcase units could house a typewriter or a small radio. Rhode's chairs were constructed on a bentwood frame. He went on to work for Herman Miller in the late 1930s and designed a similar range which he called a 'plan for comfortable living'. His philosophy, which suggested that furniture dic-

A range of pieces from Gilbert Rhode's 'Living-Dining-Sleeping' group of furniture items produced by the Kroehler Manufacturing Company in the early 1930s to meet the needs of the inhabitants of the modestly sized homes constructed in that decade.

tated the entire life-style of the person who bought it, was in keeping with the ideals of the European founders of the Modern Movement who saw in the modern style the opportunity of a reformed life-style of efficiency and social equality. Rhode made those ideas widely available in the USA in the 1930s.

The need for flexibility reduced

the number of suites of furniture – whether for the bedroom, the dining-room or the drawing-room – which American consumers bought in the 1930s. Up until then everything for the mass market had come in suites in the USA, as in most European countries. Now, furniture could be bought in individual pieces. In the words of Martin Grief: *"appearance of sectional furniture offered flexibility to a depressed industry and economy to a consumer who could now only infrequently afford the purchase of an entire matching suite"*.

The Herman Miller Company, had been set up in 1932 by a certain D.J. de Pree who started by making authentic reproduction furniture. The constant pressure from salesmen for new lines caused de Pree to think about modern furniture and he became more interested in the idea when, in the late 1920s, he saw an exhibition of French modern pieces. When Rhode, a former photographer and commercial illustrator, suggested designing some modern bedroom suites for Miller the company was very receptive to the offer and took him on board immediately. At first de Pree was displeased with Rhode's designs, which he called 'vocational school furniture' but he was quickly won over by the designer's insistence that this was the way of the future.

Although simple modern furniture emerged simultaneously from a number of different quarters in the USA it was not received immediately with unanimous approval. The Modern style appeared first in public places – cocktail bars, hotel foyers and cinemas – before it infiltrated the home, and then it was found in the kitchen before it finally entered the living-room. Its emergence in this last area was not achieved without a high degree of encouragement from 'taste-makers', salesmen, and exhibitions in galleries and department stores, and even then it only ever reached the middle class sector of the total market. While Winifred Fales, in her book *What's New in Home Decorating* of 1936 wholeheartedly recommended Rhode's range of furniture, she also praised the qualities of *"chairs of Windsor ladder-back, or Georgian types"* and a Welsh dresser, which she claimed would *"make a picturesque addition to the room providing it is in harmony with the furnishings as a whole"*. Where the mantel was concerned, she maintained that, *"it may be of any style and period you choose, from the florid carved oak of the Tudors up through the centuries to the chaste simplicity of Colonial marble or white-painted wood or the modernism of modern glass"*, proving that stylistic eclecticism was still much encouraged in this period.

Where popular taste was concerned, this mixture of period styles was undoubtedly still the norm, and was mirrored, inevitably, by the output of most of the furniture factories. Things had not changed fundamentally since the turn of the century, except that some of the stylistic options had simply been substituted for others.

Where change did occur, however, both in reproduction and modern pieces, was in the use of new materials and techniques as a means of keeping costs down. 'Flexwood' – a wood veneer mounted on to a flexible canvas backing and used to cover walls – was just one instance. Veneer-covered laminated wood was also increasingly used in this period for cabinet and table construction, in order to allow cheap, standardized production. Other materials such as glass, cork, asbestos and aluminium were introduced mostly as novel alternatives to wood.

In the end, in spite of the attempts to democratize the modern style in the USA in the 1930s, it was only accepted by one sector of the market and then, not as *the* style, but simply as one of the alternatives. It wasn't yet seen as an American style but, (like the 18th-century furniture which still pre-occupied upper class taste) as European. After the Second World War this was to change radically and in the years after 1940 it became possible, for the first time, to talk about a modern furniture style whose origins were wholly American.

6

BRITISH FURNITURE
OF
REACTION

WRITING in 1947 in their book *Modern Applied Art*, Rudolph and Helena Ratzka observed that *"to judge from the similarity of English and American experiences, the delay (in adopting the modern style) was due in great measure to the manufacturers, who were reluctant to invest in the costly models, dies and merchandizing of a new type of design so long as business was satisfactory"*. The same argument is frequently put forward today as the main reason why British furniture was, and still is, so essentially conservative in nature. As with the USA the determination to industrialize furniture making at all costs brought with it a reactionary attitude towards design. The nature of the market is clearly also of vital importance in this context. Reasons such as the fact that *"a wealthy and victorious nation has no incentive for changing its established modes and habits"* were voiced from across the Atlantic. Whatever the reason, Britain, along with the USA, was well behind Germany, Austria and the Scandinavian countries in responding to the advantages of modern furniture in the inter-war years. It seemed unable to renew the energies for innovative and creative furniture design that it had last experienced in the 18th century.

This is not to dismiss the importance of what did occur in Britain in this period, however. The particular routes that British industry took to meet the requirements of its home market support wholeheartedly the central thesis of this book i.e. that modern furniture for the mass market has developed through a tension between innovation and conservatism.

Furniture buying in Britain in the inter-war years was related directly to the concept of the 'home'. Huge numbers of houses, public and private, were built in this period, and the occupants of these new premises provided the furniture industry with its main clients. The new housing was centred either within local authority developments (where semi-detached or terraced houses were built in the style of the late Arts and Crafts Movement or Garden City architecture), or it formed part of the new suburban ribbon developments, which consisted of semi-detached 'villas' in Modern, Tudor or Arts and Crafts styles. Neither the style of this housing nor the interior plans, which showed the conventional separation of the living from the dining area, encouraged a break with tradition in the choice of furniture. The vast majority of pieces bought for housing of this type came in suites, whether for the dining- or the living-room.

It has also been estimated that, in 1932, 80 per cent of people's preferences were for period furniture. Since the 19th century the British furniture manufacturers had continued to expand their markets gradually, as a means of economic survival, to include lower and lower income groups. Where taste was concerned, however, it was the middle class market that still set the pace, and as a result period style ruled the day.

The industry, still based predominantly in Shoreditch and High Wycombe, had no other ambition than to meet demand, and so it continued to produce dining suites (a table, six chairs and sideboard); living room suites (an upholstered sofa and two upholstered chairs); and bedroom suites (a bed, a wardrobe, a chest of drawers and a dressing table). In *The Studio Yearbook* of 1929 a suite was defined as *"certain standardized units which have become traditional and which it suits the purpose of the trade to maintain as a convenient basis for governing production and distribution"*. It was undoubtedly easier to attract customers into a shop which displayed whole suites of furniture rather than isolated pieces which got lost in the window or showroom. Also, with the increasing custom of buying on credit or hire purchase, the furniture retailers needed large sums of money flowing through their businesses to survive.

Standardization had entered the British trade, and it became in the 1930s an essential question for the industry to confront in order to increase its output, lower prices and reach a larger market.

Although the general public was totally committed to the notion of the standardized suite, which had been firmly established since the 19th century, it was less happy about keeping to a narrow range of styles. Traditional furniture design offered a choice of style, and people wanted their homes to show some signs of individualism. It was important,

A British sitting room containing numerous furniture items from the 1930s including a heavy three-piece suite upholstered in leather which became a popular set of items in the newly-constructed semi-detached homes of that decade.

therefore, that, although all houses were planned in more or less the same way and everybody bought the same furniture types, there should be plenty of variation among the models available.

The furniture manufacturers had, as a result, to combine standardization with variation. They did this by, for example, making sideboards (sold as part of the dining suites) with a range of different door-shapes, handles, plinths and carved decorations. In her excellent study of popular British furniture in the 1930s Suzette Worden examined a range of sideboards produced between 1933 and 1939 by E. Gomme, a firm which had opened its large new factory in High Wycombe in 1925 and which manufactured what was called 'medium-grade' furniture. She discovered that, out of the sample she examined, 47 different models were produced, based on only seven basic carcases. The styles offered varied from period ones to others based loosely on modern idioms, many of them influenced by

A suite of dining-room furniture produced and sold by Bowman Brothers of Camden Town in the 1930s.

the geometric forms which originated in France and which could be copied directly from French pattern-books.

Where three-piece living-room suites were concerned it was easy to include variety by using different textiles and by varying the shapes achieved by the upholstery. This was still, at that time, executed entirely by hand and was therefore infinitely variable. Both the sideboard and the three-piece suite were important status objects in the home, providing luxury, comfort and individualism for people who still derived their values from older aristocratic models.

In spite of this essential conservatism there was a gradual move, from the 1920s into the 1930s, both in sideboards and upholstered furniture, away from period and towards modern styles. There were several reasons for this. One was the growing impact of propaganda from bodies like the Design and Industries Association (which promoted the modern, functional style embraced by Germany), and the influence of exhibitions and magazine articles extolling the virtues of the modern style. In addition, the increasing availability of new materials, such as plywood

and blockwood, combined with the rational 'flow' production adopted in many factories, meant that it became much easier to produce furniture with flush finishes, without detailed carving or ornamentation. The use of veneers provided whatever decoration was called for, and patterns such as the well-known sun-ray motif appeared on the flat wooden surfaces of a number of furniture pieces in the 1930s. Companies such as Furniture Industries Limited (later renamed Ercol) in High Wycombe, and Goodearl Risboro, based in Princes Risborough, supplied this type of furniture in huge numbers.

While the new laminated woods encouraged some stylistic changes during this period, there was little innovation within the factories themselves. The same machines that had been installed in the second half of the 19th century remained as the mainstay, although a number were improved, some combination machines were introduced, and electrical drive made things easier.

One significant innovation in British popular furnishings of the 1930s was the small, wooden-armed, lightly upholstered fireside chair, which replaced the traditional Windsor chair, the 'Gossip' or the small cane chair in working class kitchens. As this was a new furniture-type it was completely acceptable for its appearance to be novel as well. It

SUPREME VALUES IN HIDE THREE-PIECE SUITES

THE "CHELSEA" THREE-PIECE SUITE

THE "TRURO" THREE-PIECE SUITE

SETTEE, Sale Price **£5.15.0**
EASY CHAIR, Sale Price **£4.12.6**

A Three-Piece Suite of very comfortable and modern design. Upholstered in good quality hide with outside backs and sides in Rexine. Loose spring cushions covered in Brown velveteen. A Suite to stand hard wear Settee 4 ft. 9 in. wide Easy Chairs 33 in. wide Depth of seats 24 in

THE THREE PIECES—
SALE PRICE **£13.15.0** Or 27/6 with order, and 12 months payments of 21/2

2 ft. 6 in. WALNUT
COCKTAIL CABINET

With automatic opening top. Containing 19 pieces of glassware, cocktail shaker, lemon squeezer, knife, spoon and cherry picks. Storage cupboard below

SALE PRICE **10** GUINEAS

Or 21/- with order, and 12 monthly payments of 16/1 Also in Mahogany or Oak at the same price.

SETTEE, Sale Price **£5.**
EASY CHAIR, Sale Price **£3.1**

A comfortably upholst outside backs and side Rexine, and velveteen Pu spring cushions. The S is 4 ft. 8 in. wide. Easy Chairs 32 in. wide. Depth of seats 22 in

THE THREE PIECES—
SALE PRICE **£12.10.0** Or 24/- with order, and 12 mo payments of 19/4

OETZMANN & CO. LTD.   Telephone EUSton 5(

A page from a catalogue issued in the early 1930s by the London-based furniture retailer Oetzmann and Company Limited showing two of its three-piece suites upholstered in hide and completed with velveteen cushions.

emerged as a small, simple undecorated item with open forms closely resembling European examples of the same year. The major technological advance which enabled the fireside chair to be so light and comfortable was the discovery, by the German, Willy Knoll, of tension springs which replaced the steel coils of earlier upholstered chairs. Knoll brought his invention with him to Britain when he left Stuttgart in the 1930s, and he designed a range of fireside chairs which were manufactured by the High Wycombe firm, F. Parker and Sons Limited, under the name of Parker-Knoll. They quickly became highly popular and brought the British public as near as it was to go in that period towards the idea of modern furniture.

The other notable technological breakthrough of the period was the invention, by the Dunlop Rubber Company, of 'Dunlopillo' – a latex foam used in cushions. It was not to have much effect on domestic furniture, however, until a little later, although it was used widely for car and bus seats before 1939.

Although there was *some* evidence in Britain of the influence of the advances made in the USA and on the Continent in the inter-war years, this tended to be evident only in an upper middle class context, rather than at the mass market level. Built-in, unit and dual-purpose furniture was available only from such up-market retail outlets as Heal's and Bowman's. Avant-garde architects, such as Serge Chermayeff and Wells Coates, and interior decorators in the French tradition, such as J. Duncan Miller, also used these flexible pieces in their fashionable modern interiors.

The way tubular steel furniture was received in Britain reveals much about British attitudes at this time. As a domestic item it never penetrated beyond the most fashionable of interiors, and it seemed to repel the British public through its coldness, its austerity, its complete break with the craft tradition of woodworking, and its aggressive modernity. The English writer, Herbert Read, summed up this innate suspicion and conservatism in his book *Art and Industry* in which he claimed that *"new materials for furniture-making or a new and unsuspected use of familiar materials are inclined to disturb our sense of structural propriety"*. Cartoonists such as Osbert Lancaster and Heath Robinson mocked without mercy the pretentiousness associated with tubular steel furniture. Only the most avant-garde architects (who modelled themselves on their Continental counterparts) ever allowed such furniture into their homes, and the

majority of tubular steel pieces were relegated instead to cinema foyers and village halls.

It was in the very early 1930s that PEL (Practical Equipment Limited), which had developed originally from a company called Tube Investments, first introduced tubular steel into Britain, and its early models were shameless imitations of earlier Thonet designs. Commissions received by the company included furnishing Broadcasting House which gave the firm a great deal of coverage in the press. This was quickly followed by orders to furnish a number of smart hotels including the Metropole in Brighton. PEL furniture was retailed through

the same shops which stocked unit furniture but, by the middle of the decade, it had begun to break loose from its 'ultra-modern' associations and to become more commercial in its appeal. The designs became efficient-looking rather than fashionable, and the simple PEL stacking chair, the RP6, with its canvas seat and back, is probably the best known and remembered of all its models.

One of the reasons why the British avant-garde rejected tubular steel, (apart from the fact that the pieces were more expensive than their wooden equivalents), was because they were growing infatuated, by the mid 1930s, with the bent plywood

Ian Henderson's living-room in a small flat, designed for Miss Jeanne de Casalis, contains built-in furniture made of ash and walnut.

Above: A Parker-Knoll brochure from the late 1930s showing the application of that company's covered horizontal coil springs which radically altered attitudes towards upholstery in that period.

furniture being imported from Finland by firms such as Finmar. This proved much more suited to a public which had been brought up under the influence of the Arts and Crafts Movement.

By the 1930s, plywood was widely used as a substitute for solid wood for such features as the backs of wardrobes and the bottoms of shelves in chests of drawers. Furniture made entirely of bent ply and laminated wood, however, remained the preserve of the avant-garde and middle class market, both because it smacked of 'Modernism' and because it had originated on the Continent. Marcel Breuer came to Britain in the mid 1930s and worked with the architect Jack Pritchard on a range of

A set of walnut dining-room furniture designed by R.D. Russell and manufactured by Gordon Russell Limited in the 1930s: the table has moulded legs and the chairs are covered in a blue tapestry.

furniture made of bent plywood. Sold through Pritchard's company, Isokon, it was popular among British intellectuals of the period.

Sweden also had a major influence on some types of furniture at this time, particularly on the work and ideas of Gordon Russell, who was a major figure within the latter-day British Arts and Crafts Movement of the 1920s and 30s. Russell emerged from the same Cotswold traditions that had produced other major Arts and Crafts protagonists such as Ernest Gimson and the Barnsley Brothers but, unlike his predecessors, Russell was convinced of the role that machines were to play in 20th-century furniture. His designs from the inter-war years, produced by his firm in Broadway, Worcestershire,

Below: PEL Limited's chromium-plated tubular steel-framed table with a solid walnut top, complete with a set of six dining chairs in tubular steel upholstered in hide. Designed in the 1930s, the set only found its way into fairly avant-garde interiors.

A dining table and chairs in birch ply designed in about 1937 by Marcel Breuer for Jack Pritchard's company, Isokon.

reflected a dual interest in the traditions and image of craftsmanship and the use of the machine. While reproduction furniture was anathema to him he respected, like the Scandinavians, the virtues of scale and proportion seen in 18th-century furniture, and he translated them into his essentially modern designs. Where materials were concerned, Russell was an arch-traditionalist and he wrote extensively about the virtues of British oak, the most established of all British furniture materials.

During the pre-Second World War period, Russell reflected the essential conservatism within British society and its continued belief that there was a possible compromise between craft and machine production.

In *The Studio* magazine's *Decorative Art Yearbook* of 1939, the section on furniture featured, among other pieces, a divan by Gordon Russell Limited; an aluminium and 'Lucite' chair by the American W.D. Teague; and work by the Scandinavian designers Bruno Mathsson and Carl Malmsten. The furniture types illustrated ranged from unit bookcases to bars, to radio cabinets to more conventional tables and chairs. A sense of internationalism was gradually penetrating the previously rather parochial world of British furniture. Admittedly at that time, it was a tendency which affected only the wealthier sector of the market, but after the War, both the cultural and the economic frameworks of furniture production in Britain were to alter radically.

PART THREE

POST-WAR RECONSTRUCTION (1940-1960)

"Today war-time production has accelerated interest in all kinds of plastic substances. Modern aeroplane production has shown that flexible wood, pliant glass and many composite metals and substances can be mass-produced.....undoubtedly these new materials will be used in the home".

Derek Patmore *Colour Schemes and Modern Furnishings 1945*

IN the years after 1945 furniture played a major role in the cultural and economic regeneration of a number of countries which had been devastated by the War. The aesthetic and the production processes of the modern furniture styles had been well established by the years before 1939 and they had, to some extent, penetrated the mass market. However, it was the new technology which came out of the War that made it possible, for the first time, for mass produced furniture to confront the modern age head on.

Among the numerous advances achieved by war research were developments in plywood technology, as applied to aircraft construction. Strong water-proof plywoods, in particular, were developed in this period as well as wood which didn't swell and shrink. Aluminium and magnesium, the light metals, were made more available than ever before, as was stainless steel. Perhaps most significantly of all, however, plastics technology reached a new level of sophistication. One aspect of this was the development of new synthetic resins, used to bond materials together. None of those researches took place within the furniture industry itself, which had mostly either stopped producing or gone over to war work, but after the war the new ideas were ready and waiting to be applied to furniture manufacture. They had the effect of changing the face of modern furniture irrevocably.

During the War years buying furniture was clearly not a priority, although in the case of young marrieds and the owners of bombed houses it was still a necessity. Special provisions were made in a number of countries for these particular needs, in the form of state controlled furniture production. This had radical effects on the public's attitude towards furniture, both during and after the War, not least because the imposed authority created a deep-seated reaction, and a sudden wish for more expressive furniture.

In the immediate post-war years, Europe's previous lead in furniture culture was rapidly overtaken by the USA, mainly as a result of the advances it had made both technologically and aesthetically during the War years. It had had time to absorb the European developments of the inter-war period and to consolidate its own position. Soon, however, Scandinavia, and later Italy, were to re-establish the dominance of Europe in the international furniture market.

The period after 1945 is characterized by much stronger international communication than ever before. The War had broken down national insularity for all time, and cultural influences flowed freely across national barriers. In this period, or at least by the end of it, it became possible to talk realistically about the mass consumption of furniture in most countries of the industrialized world. Ideas about furniture, and technical innovations, moved quickly not only from country to country (helped by exhibitions, such as the Triennales in Milan, and the expanding number of specialist magazines) but also through the social barriers in the same country. As a result the gaps between the different levels of the market shrank, and modern furniture penetrated the popular imagination for the first time. No longer was there such a wide gulf between mass produced furniture and the work of the progressive designers.

The period 1940-1960 is one of expansion, for the furniture industry and for furniture retailing. It is also the period in which some of the most exciting advances in the evolution of modern furniture for the mass market were achieved.

Verner Panton's cantilevered chair made from a single moulded glass-fibre shell. It was designed in 1960 but not produced by Herman Miller until 1967.

7

AMERICA: TECHNIQUE AND INNOVATION

"We have been watching the advertisements, the movies and the magazines and the swing to the modern has definitely begun".

George Nelson *Tomorrow's House* **1945**

GEORGE Nelson's comment marked the beginning of a realization that, in the USA modern furniture was no longer limited to a rather esoteric market but was now available en masse, and had even become associated, in the public's mind, with the newly emerging post-war society.

The decade immediately following the Second World War was one in which the mass production of furniture in the USA expanded enormously and America also took the lead in new design. The increase in production came about as a result of the manufacturers having to streamline their methods, to help with the War effort, and as a result of the mammoth building programmes which were set up to deal with the housing shortage created by the War. The innovations in design were a direct spin-off of technologies developed and perfected during the War. Suddenly the USA ceased to be preoccupied exlusively with European style and it began instead to create, produce and buy mass market furniture which, although not totally disassociated from European models, belonged more firmly to an American context than ever before. A new level of confidence, on the part of the designer, the manufacturer and the consumer, had reversed the coin and, in a number of instances, Europe began to emulate the achievements of the USA.

In Italy, Britain and Scandinavia, for instance, the work of America's best known furniture designer of this period, Charles Eames, filled the pages of specialist design and furniture magazines in the late 1940s and by the 1950s he had replaced Le Corbusier, Mies van der Rohe and Alvar Aalto as the most internationally revered furniture designer of the day.

The story of American furniture after 1940 is, however, a much more complex and interesting one than the study of the work of a few of the heroes of the period would suggest. The work of these figures remained, for the most part, the privilege of an élite, and was more at home in museums than in the domestic settings of the new suburbanites. The latter were more likely to be buying either reproduction American Colonial furniture or Grand Rapids' versions of modern furniture pieces, which bore only vague resemblances to their avant-garde inspirers.

The international success of American furniture innovation in this period was due as much to the pioneering efforts of a small number of manufacturing firms as to those of a handful of individual designers. In 1947 the industry was the second largest producer of consumer goods in the USA. It was scattered throughout 45 of the 47 states and comprised about 3,500 manufacturers in total, many of them fairly small-scale operations.

While Grand Rapids, Chicago and the other traditional areas were still the major centres, producing a huge variety of styles, they were being increasingly challenged by companies in North Carolina and on the West Coast. The availability of cheap labour in these locations meant that factories could make even cheaper goods and cater for the varied tastes of the new consumers. As a result of this increasing competition Grand Rapids began to concentrate more than ever on goods of a higher quality aimed at a slightly wealthier market. They left the really low income groups to the Southern manufacturers which, in 1947, provided 30 per cent of the wooden household furniture made in the USA. In 1947 George Nelson commented that , *"The South turns out an appalling quantity of the worst kind of furniture"*. Companies in the South like Broyhill and Bassett Industries were producing 'borax' furniture – i.e. that of the lowest possible taste and quality. Most of the companies operated on a modest, low investment basis, but there were a few exceptions, notably the Kroehler manufacturing company (which had, in 1947, nine plants in the USA and Canada) and the Mengel Company.

The Mengel Company had worked on a number of other products including wood boxes and automobile bodies, before moving on to the large-scale production of veneers and furniture plywood. Before taking this change in direction it carried out a great deal of market research and advertising, finally deciding on a range of products intended 'to offend as few people as possible'.

The general picture was one of a multitude of small companies producing a huge variety of furniture styles ranging from period to borax to modern, aimed at an ever bigger and lower income market. There were signs, however, in the immediate post-war years, that a few isolated companies were prepared to give the

Eero Saarinen's 'Womb' chair and footstool designed originally in 1948 and manufactured later by Knoll. The bases are made from steel tubing and the seat from moulded plastic with foam-rubber upholstery.

public what they felt was right, rather than simply fulfilling the supposed requirements of mass taste. A programme to encourage 'taste' discrimination, undertaken through a mass of publications and through institutions like the Museum of Modern Art in New York, backed up their efforts. The firms included the Baker Furniture company (which commissioned the Dane Finn Juhl to design its showroom in this period), H.G. Knoll, Herman Miller and the Widdicomb company. All of them chose to stake their futures on the conviction that there was a market for modern furniture of top design quality.

Another important factor in the post-war period was the effect created by war-time work in certain furniture companies on aircraft components. This had meant a massive reduction of furniture lines and the introduction of new techniques, such as moulding plywood and electric gluing. The increased standardization and technical sophistication achieved by these firms put them in a very strong position at the end of the War to experiment with progressive furniture forms.

The furniture pieces with moulded plywood shell seats and backs designed by Charles Eames and Eero Saarinen in 1940 were a prime example of the use of advanced manufacturing techniques applied to furniture design and production.

A lounge chair and ottoman with a moulded rosewood shell and leather cover designed by Charles Eames as a TV chair for the playwright Billy Wilder and manufactured by Herman Miller in 1956.

A comprehensive storage system designed by George Nelson for Herman Miller in 1959 with a moulded plywood chair by Charles Eames.

Eero Saarinen's pedestal furniture, including the 'Tulip' chair with a moulded plastic seat and covered metal pedestal designed for Knoll in 1956.

Dining and lounge height chairs in moulded plywood designed by Charles and Ray Eames and produced by Herman Miller in 1946.

Their all wooden pieces first entered the public arena when they were shown at an exhibition for the prize-winners of a competition organized by the Museum of Modern Art in New York. This was followed by an exhibition of Eames' designs in 1946, the year in which he first joined metal legs to a moulded wood shell with the addition of rubber shock mounts. An article in *Arts and Architecture* commented that *"Eames has designed and produced the most important group of furniture ever developed in this country. His achievement is a compound of aesthetic brilliance and technical inventiveness"*. The earlier pieces, which combined moulded ply seats and backs with laminated wood legs, had been planned for production by a firm called Evans Products. This was a large firm in the Mengel mould, which had previously worked in both wood and metal, and had made, among other products, parts for metal oil burners. Evans died before this project could get off the ground, but in 1946 Eames was introduced to the Herman Miller company by George Nelson. Miller had already established its forward looking attitude towards modern design through its work with Gilbert Rhode in the 1930s. Its relationship with Eames turned out to be both longstanding and highly profitable.

At the top end of the market, companies like Herman Miller and Knoll (the latter took on board the designs of Eero Saarinen in the 1950s) were providing pieces which put America on the furniture design map. At the same time the American mass market was also beginning to include more modern furniture items in its homes, albeit usually cheaper versions of the originals. There were a number of reasons for this. The most obvious was the huge increase in the construction of standardized suburban housing in the post-war period and the natural desire of its occupants to equip their homes with new and appropriate furniture. Many newly built suburban towns, such as Lewittown for instance, were made up completely of ranch-style houses and, according to Russel Lynes, *"the standardized house creates an emphasis on interior decorating. Most people try hard to achieve something different"*. Lynes isolated two main interior styles that emerged in the period, labelling them 'Early American' and 'Modern', and he explained that the inspiration for the styles came predominantly from films, TV and national magazines such as *Good Housekeeping* and *Ladies Home Journal*. Regional taste varied less in this period as a result of mass communications – to the extent that the Sears Roebuck company was now able to publish just one catalogue, instead of the previous six.

The Modern, or, as it came to be called, the 'Contemporary', interior design and furniture style that the suburbanites adopted was described by George Nelson as *"The plywood and rubber-plant school of design"*. It consisted in essence, of watered-down versions of the furniture pieces that top pace-setter designers like Charles Eames, Eero Saarinen, Harry Bertoia, Isamu Noguchi, Paul Laszlo, Ed Wormley and others were producing in this period. The pieces responded to certain practical requirements such as the diminishing space in most homes, which inevitably influenced furniture size and storage facilities. Many things could now be stored in the kitchen, which had become more efficiently organized, and so there was no longer a need for sideboards or, indeed, wardrobes which were replaced increasingly by built-in cupboards.

In his book *Tomorrow's House*, in which he outlined many of the ideas that determined the popular decoration and furniture styles of the post-war period, George Nelson explained how the 'Contemporary' house got rid of the 'little partitioned cubicles called rooms'; stored all its essential equipment at the wall in built-in stor-

George Nelson's 'Basic Storage Components' designed for the Herman Miller Company in 1949, were one of the earliest examples of a complete wall storage system of this kind.

age systems; and encouraged maximum flexibility in its choice of furniture. With the removal of traditional pieces of storage furniture, the number of items in a house was effectively reduced and the 'sitting-object' took on a new significance, isolated as it was in the middle of an open space which had all its storage at the walls. The chair took on, inevitably, a more overtly sculptural role as it was forced into this new position.

Nelson also described the concept of the kitchen/dining room (an early example of which had been exhibited at the New York World's Fair in 1939) and emphasized the fact that traditional furniture – in particular light pieces like the Windsor chair – could be incorporated into what he called 'the contemporary interior of the shrinking house'.

The new emphasis on the silhouette of the chair encouraged many experiments with form in these years. Lightness, transparency and elegance became priorities in this new 'spacious' environment, and this in turn led to the use of glass and light metals. These materials were also being widely used in house construction and the large expanses of glass and open spaces thus created made the heavy furniture of the Victorian period and the 1930s look inappropriate. Chairs and coffee tables became instead more organic and sculptural to contrast with the strict

The sculptor Harry Bertoia's 'Grid' chair 1952, was made of steel rod, either chrome plated or plastic coated, and came with a padded seat in either cotton or leather.

rectilinear forms of the storage units which hugged the walls. In 1953 Nelson wrote that 'while sofas are becoming built-in seating, chairs are becoming pieces of sculpture' and this tendency became increasingly pronounced as it moved down market. As the 'Contemporary' style became increasingly popular, manufacturers sought ever new ways of making sculptural shapes out of modern industrial materials, aided by the manufacturing techniques that had come out of war-time research. The more overtly stylized furniture style became, the more the top designers disassociated themselves from it.

Many of them compared it to the 'Georgian or French provincial settings faked up by the decorators for the more prosperous suburbanites.'

By the mid 1950s modern furniture, in some form or another, had become accepted by a large section of the mass market. Many manufacturers, inspired by the successes of firms like Miller and Knoll, had moved away from their preoccupation with wood and had invested in new machinery to work the new materials. Modern furniture became, increasingly, a mark of 'taste and social status replacing the reproduction pieces of yesteryear.' Originality became a by-word and manufacturers went to great lengths to combine, for instance, coffee-tables, plant holders and magazine racks in new ways.

The growing popularity of the modern style added to the USA's ascendancy in the area of furniture design, and much money and effort was put into promoting the American achievement. The Museum of Modern Art included numerous pieces of Knoll and Herman Miller furniture in its 'Good Design' exhibitions of the early 1950s and countless magazines made them available to those who could not see them at first hand. Along with its financial aid, the USA also exported to Europe an enthusiasm for modern furniture and inspired a number of other countries to revitalize their own interest.

8

CRAFT AND INDUSTRY IN SCANDINAVIA

IT was in the post-war period that Scandinavian furniture burst onto the international market and captured the popular imagination in a major way. It provided the ideal model of the domestic interior for a number of different reasons. Firstly, it rejected the harsh forms of functionalism that many people associated with the hard years of the 1930s. Through its light forms and decorative surfaces, it communicated instead an essentially optimistic and human aesthetic which pointed the way forward out of austerity It was a friendly style which combined the past with the future and expressed a democratic approach towards living – an important factor for a world which had just witnessed the ravages of totalitarianism. For all these and other reasons Scandinavian domestic design became increasingly fashionable internationally in the years between 1940 and 1960. In the mid 1950s an exhibition of Scandinavian objects toured the USA leaving behind it a trail of enthusiasm. The pages of design and furniture magazines the world over began to reflect the growing international obsession with things Scandinavian.

The contributions of Denmark, Sweden and Finland were, however, quite distinct one from the other. The country which merits the greatest attention is undoubtedly Denmark, from where, in the minds of many, all good furniture came in this period. Probably the strongest lasting image of Scandinavian design in the 1950s is the teak furniture that was exported in large quantities around the globe. This was a fashion for which the Danes were responsible. Supplies of teak were made available by the war with Indo-China, during which forests were felled to make room for roads to transport war equipment. Denmark made extensive use of this teak to produce and export high quality furniture, such as light wooden-armed chairs and bookcases which doubled as room dividers.

There was much more to post-war Danish furniture, however, than an obsession with teak. Its success was due mainly to its associations with tradition, craftsmanship and quality. In addition, the Danes, along with the Swedes, had been able to evolve highly practical, light pieces of furniture which could be sold singly rather than in sets, and which were ideally suited to the new, smaller living spaces. The practicality and comfort of much Danish furniture from these years harked back to the pre-war influence of Kaare Klint and to the war-time experiments of his pupil Borge Mogensen.

Mogensen was employed by the Danish Co-Operative Society between 1942 and 1950, during which he developed his ranges of simple wooden furniture for the smaller living space. Most of his interior sets were intended to fit into two rooms – the size of half the flats in Copen-

A simple, country-inspired light wood chair with a rush seat designed by Borge Mogensen for the Danish Co-operative Society in the 1940s.

ments of his pieces scientifically, making sure that they could fit into his two-roomed experimental flat.

The second 20th-century Danish tradition – the co-operation of the furniture architect with the cabinet-maker – was also put to the test in the post-war period, most notably in the work of Hans Wegner who became, for many, the best known Danish furniture designer of this century. He is most famous for his chair design of 1949, referred to simply, and with a great sense of reverence, as 'The Chair'. It was an unpretentious design which combined a traditional material (beechwood) with ergo-

nomic precision and a modern sculptured look. Wegner's work, including a number of other chairs which have since become 'classics', served to demonstrate the continued importance of the Danish cabinet-maker as well as the new move, in the 1950s, from a scientific to a more openly expressive type of furniture design.

The 1950s were, in many ways the years of cabinet-makers and joiners in Denmark, as there was a strong international market for their exclusive furniture. The workshop of Johannes Hansen worked with Wegner from 1950 onwards – it was a family firm

Sculptural teak and leather two-seater sofa designed in the late 1950s by Finn Juhl. It illustrates Juhl's use of the 'floating seat' for which he became renowned in that decade.

hagen at that time – and combined the functions of different activities – such as sleeping with relaxing, and eating with working. Mogensen's designs depended totally upon well-known furniture types, such as the Swedish stick-back chair, the English Windsor chair and American Shaker furniture – all of which were vernacular rather than overtly stylish in origin and were noted for their functional qualities. The use of traditional types gave Mogensen's pieces a sense of familiarity and domesticity. The pieces could be bought individually as well as in sets. Like Klint before him, Mogensen tested the measure-

Hans Wegner's chair in solid teak designed in 1949 and known simply as 'the Chair'.

which employed a small number of highly skilled employees. Wegner's 1949 chair was made out of solid wood, which was kept on the premises in log form for two years, to make sure it was completely dry, before it was put together and hand-finished in the workshop. The other principal protagonist in the story of 1950s Danish furniture was a younger man, Finn Juhl, in whose work the expressive possibility of solid wood furniture came into its own. The twin influences of African tribal sculpture and contemporary organic sculpture were combined in his new furniture aesthetic. The exclusive and luxurious nature of Danish furniture in the 1950s was nowhere more apparent than in the work of the architect Poul

Kjaerholm. Although he was committed to industrial materials, particularly steel, he developed an elegant aesthetic far removed from Mogensen's democratic concerns.

At the same time as the cabinet makers were producing these exclusive designs, other parts of the Danish furniture industry were developing the route of mass production. Danish furniture manufacturing had never been fully industrialized in the American sense of the word but, in the postwar years, the increasing demands of the world market made it possible for Denmark to consider production on a scale larger than ever before. The company of Fritz Hansen was the most successful example.

Fritz Hansen, a cabinet-maker by profession, had initially set up his business in 1872, specializing in wood-turning. His later interest in bentwood had encouraged the firm to follow Thonet by bringing in a number of architects throughout the 1930s. Hansen was practically the only manufacturer to embrace functionalism in Denmark in those years (the company produced Klint's church chair in 1936), and in 1932 he began what was to turn into a long relationship with the Danish architect, Arne Jacobsen. In 1952 Jacobsen designed his 'Ant' chair for Hansen – a simple little dining-chair, the seat and back of which were pressed in one piece of two-layer veneer

and then supported on steel legs. It was a design which owed much to Eames but which went one stage further. The 'Ant' was followed by two upholstered chairs called the 'Egg' and the 'Swan' which became familiar in many fashionable interiors in the 1950s. Jacobsen was developing Saarinen's idea of seeing the chair as a kind of 'womb' which both encapsulates and protects its sitter. It was a very different concept from the one expressed by the open structured metal tube chair of the 1920s and 1930s, made possible by the new techniques available for moulding

Arne Jacobsen's little 'Ant' chair designed for Fritz Hansen in 1952 made from beech plywood. The seat and back are moulded in a single piece.

The 'Swan' easy-chair was designed by Arne Jacobsen for Fritz Hansen in 1957. Its plastic shell is rendered more comfortable with the addition of foam rubber upholstery.

laminated wood and fibre-glass.

The other Danish designer of note from these years was Verner Panton, best known perhaps for his one-piece cantilevered plastic chair. This was an innovation that he made ahead even of the Americans and Italians, who were so advanced in plastics research. While Danish industry was pushing forward the possibilities of new production techniques within furniture manufacture, it remained always careful to sustain its hard-earned reputation for 'quality', whether of craftsmanship or of design. Danish innovations were copied widely and became, in the mass market sectors of many countries, inextricably linked with the idea of the 'contemporary' interior.

Sweden was also a strong international influence in the post-war years, concentrating its efforts on measuring the size of flats and estimating the ideal size and proportions of furni-

An interior from the 1950s by the Swedish Design AB group showing the use of a room-divider both as storage and as a means of cutting up the interior space.

ture items for the small home. In 1948 a researcher called Bengt Akerblom published a book called *Standing and Sitting Posture* which quickly became a key textbook for furniture designers internationally. In Sweden men like C.A.Acking and Axel Larssen were strongly influenced by it and designed ranges of light, wooden chairs based on the strict anthropometric measurements it proposed.

As in Denmark, the consequences of war-time standard furniture and of the Co-operative movement were important in Sweden. Gordon Russell commented that the latter organization was unique in 'deciding that its customers were intelligent'. Among the most interesting and influential new developments was the range of 'Package' furniture that Elias Svedberg designed for the Stockholm department store, Nordiska Kompaniet, just after the war. These designs showed a new approach to the problems of storage and of transporting furniture between the manufacturer, the retail outlet and the final destination. The idea provided the basis of 'knock-down' furniture which became increasingly popular internationally after the Second World War. Svedberg's furniture was brought to Britain just after the War and was widely seen, admired and emulated at a time when government-controlled 'Utility' furniture was still the only thing being produced.

While Denmark was noted for particular 'classics' of modern furniture design, Sweden's commitment was to the practicality and comfort of the whole domestic environment, achieved by mixing traditional with new items. Windsor chairs and pine beds, which recalled 17th-century Swedish models, were combined with novel and practical furniture pieces such as sets of nesting tables, trolleys and stacking chairs. The main emphasis was upon making the small interior seem as spacious, light, comfortable and human as possible. Pine and birch were the dominant woods and the Swedish interiors, illustrated through the 1950s in international glossy magazines, invariably included a bowl of fresh flowers, books on the shelves, small ornaments on the cabinets and people sitting reading on the chairs.

The pioneering work of men like G.A. Berg, Josef Frank and Bruno Mathsson had finally come of age and reached the mass environment. The 'Swedish Modern' was one of the most important influences on the post-war international image of the home.

The Finnish contribution of the same period was less preoccupied with precise measurements and democratic idealism than that of Denmark and Sweden. Finland, nonetheless, initiated a furniture movement which became recognized internationally by the end of the 1950s. Finnish furniture was more overtly industrial and more expressive than anything Denmark or Sweden had to offer. First noticed at the Milan Triennales of the early 1950s it quickly became the favoured style of an international élite.

The Finnish phenomenon developed in the years between 1949 and 1959. There were no workshops in Finland, as there were in Denmark, and so progress lay in the hands of the furniture industry. The Asko company played a particularly important role as it was one of the earliest and largest Finnish companies to sponsor modern design. During the 1930s the company's main production had been dominated by suites, and it had actively opposed the making of furniture in prisons, which was becoming a major problem for the industry. During the War furniture production in Finland was controlled, but in the late 1940s Asko began to renew its machinery, and set out to meet the needs of the new market created by the post-war building programmes. There was considerable pressure for new models and so designers were brought in – who looked, inevitably, to Sweden for their first inspiration. In the mid 1950s Asko began making foam-rubber, called Askolette, and the interior architects employed by the firm, (Olli Borg, Ilmari Lappalainen and Ilmari Tapiovaara) were quick to exploit the potential of this new material. It was combined with both plywood and metal, and the designs which emerged had remarkably imaginative, forward-looking and elegant forms. Other notable designs from this decade include Tapiovaara's version of the Windsor chair, called 'Mademoiselle'. Designed in 1958, it showed signs of the sculptural exuberance of 'Finnish Flair' – a concept which formed part of international furniture culture by the end of the 1950s, at least for one sector of the market.

It was in the 1960s that Asko and a number of other Finnish manufacturers and individuals were to make their strongest impact on the international market by their widespread adoption of the 'Pop' aesthetic and their daring experiments with plastics and expressive, novel forms. Inevitably these radical pieces did not constitute the 'bread and butter' production of the industry, and the majority of the Finnish public continued to buy traditional pine and birch pieces. The Finnish industry, nevertheless, did realize that, in order to penetrate the world market, it had to be seen to take a progressive and experimental approach towards furniture.

By the end of the 1950s export markets were fully open for the Scandinavian furniture industry, whose products had become part of an international language of modern design. The style became highly popular in a number of countries, including Britain and the USA, and sold widely through high street shops with such evocative names as 'Svensk', 'Dansk' and 'Form'. While the pieces actually manufactured in Scandinavia commanded high prices, the image of Scandinavian furniture penetrated deeply into the heart of the mass market trade, and countless designs of Swedish and Danish inspiration rolled off the production lines in High Wycombe and elsewhere.

The Scandinavian style had the virtue of remaining fairly intact, however down market it moved, and it can be considered as the first modern mass furniture style of this century. As a furniture fashion it was not to last much beyond the mid 1960s, however, when it was replaced by the bright colours, expressive plastic forms and chic sculptural objects associated with the Italian modern furniture movement. Wood was replaced by plastic, black leather, and chrome; craft was dismissed in favour of advanced technology; and the symbolism in the popular home changed from the traditional to the futuristic. For domestic furniture, the age of humanism (temporarily at least), was at an end.

Ilmari Tapiovaara's little bentwood and moulded plywood chair designed for Asko in 1958 was among Finland's first ventures into the modern style after the Second World War.

9

THE BIRTH
OF DESIGNER FURNITURE

ITALY, in common with several other countries, had had many homes destroyed by the War and had halted all housing developments during and immediately after it. Where politics and industrialization were concerned, however, Italy's position was unique.

Ernesto Rogers (editor of *Domus*, the main mouthpiece of the early post-war period) was part of a movement that believed in continuing the pre-war programme to provide vast numbers of standardized pre-fabricated homes for the homeless. These were to be equipped with simple furniture items, such as the wood and canvas chairs designed by Carlo di Carli, Carlo Vigano, Ignazio Gardella (who presented his version of the American 'Hardoy' chair called the 'Poltrone tripoline') and Franco Albini, which were on show at an exhibition in Milan in 1946. According to Rogers, 15 million homes were needed in Italy in that year to house the homeless and the under-privileged. The other desperate need was for mass-produced small furni-

The 'Margherita' cane chair designed by Franco Albini in 1951 illustrates how one branch of post-war Italian furniture succeeded in combining craft traditions with modern, sculptural form.

ture items which could be folded and packed away when not in use. In 1949 a commentator wrote in *Design* magazine that, *"During these first years of post-war reconstruction the housing problem in Italy was so seri-*

ous that many people had to organize their living quarters as offices or studios during the daytime. Thus it came about that the Italian architects were among the first to design office furniture that would also look right in a well-planned living-room."

There was also, however, a backlash occurring against the architectural and design movement of the 1930s, because of its ambiguous relationship with Fascism.

In the very early post-war years Italy's designs were similar to those which were developing in the USA, Britain and Scandinavia – i.e. based on new materials and simple mass produced furniture. But when, in 1948, the Christian Democrats took over from the Popular Front, and Gio Ponti resumed the editorship of *Domus*, a more exclusive approach towards furniture began to emerge. By the 1950s, high quality, sophisticated furniture, aimed at the top end of the market, came to characterize much of Italy's output, which embraced a wide range of styles.

The Italian furniture industry was

dependent on small mechanized workshops. The market for their furniture was primarily foreign, and made up of small, fairly wealthy, style-conscious groups. As a result of these two factors Italian designs could stress individualism, style and variation, rather than the qualities of simplicity, function and standardization encouraged by large-scale industries in a number of other countries.

The large majority of post-war Italian furniture manufacturers were clustered around Milan, in particular in the area called Brianza, and they operated on a small-scale, often artisanal, basis. Many of them had existed as furniture workshops for a number of years, often with Austro-Hungarian roots dating back to the last century. This concentration of small industrial set-ups in one area encouraged much collaboration between them. It was fairly common practice for one firm to invest in the machinery to handle, say, plastics or metal, and then to do work for other firms on a sub-contractual basis. A few of the large firms established in these years undertook a number of different manufacturing processes, but others were simply entrepreneurial concerns, contracting out all their work, except assembly, to other companies. The variety and flexibility of the Italian furniture industry were the main reasons for its high success rate in the world market.

Italian manufacturing did not industrialize on any scale until after the War. This meant it could then buy the most advanced machinery and tools available, while countries such as Britain, which had industrialized much earlier, still used the old machinery they had originally invested in. By the early 1950s, many of the Italian firms established as workshops back in the closing years of the last century, had been rapidly reconstructed and modernized to make furniture from new materials.

Franco Albini's 'Luisa' chair of 1955 shows, in its architectural construction, the heritage of rationalism in post-war Italian design.

They were joined by a number of new companies which, free from the pressures of tradition, adopted a progressive approach towards modern furniture. The co-existence of large, medium and small firms, and the retention of handwork alongside the sophisticated new machinery, resulted in a variety and flexibility that was unmatched elsewhere. Innovation was common, and design was one of the keywords of the period.

One company which developed along a characteristic pattern in Italy was Cassina, which was established by two brothers, one of whom had been an upholsterer. In the 1920s they had specialized in cabinet-made, reproduction sewing boxes. In the following decade they moved into three-piece suites – still custom-made and in period styles of mixed origin. In the years 1947-52 the company was given a contract to supply furniture for ships, and this brought the need to expand and to move into mass production. At this point they decided to bring in an architect-designer and to start marketing modern design, rather than simply being led by the tastes of their existing clientèle. The emphasis moved from the domestic market to the world market and success became a matter of anticipating, rather than simply meeting, consumer needs. The first architect-designer Cassina worked with was Franco Albini, but its most memor-

A cabinet designed by Gio Ponti in 1950 and decorated by Piero Fornasetti.

able early collaboration was with Gio Ponti whose 'Superleggera' chair was manufactured in 1957. Designed a few years earlier, the chair, which was based on a traditional model manufactured in Chiavari near Genoa, was both elegant and modern, and small enough to be practical in the post-war interior.

The collaboration with Ponti marked the beginning of a new policy for Cassina, which involved commissioning designers to create modern pieces which would be produced in bulk and sold internationally on the basis of their refined aesthetic qualities. It was a policy which was emu-lated by numerous companies in this period. One of the factors which made it feasible was the availability of a high number of trained architects in Italy. They had little architectural work in the post-war period, due to the lack of building programmes, and were keen to apply their skills to designing architectural accessories and other consumer goods. They worked, for the most part, on a free-lance basis and were employed by the new companies who wanted to break into the world market and were seeking new forms to accompany the new materials. Cassina improved its manufacturing equipment in the post-war period and, following its successful experiment with Ponti, went on, in the 1960s, to work with numerous other designers of the day including Vico Magistretti, Tobia and Afra Scarpa, Gaetano Pesce and Mario Bellini.

Italy was commited right from the start of the post-war period, to new materials – among them bent and moulded plywood, sheet metal, steel rod, glass, foam rubber and plastics. The work of Eames and Saarinen appeared in *Domus* in the late 1940s alongside pieces of sculpture by artists such as Max Bill and Alexan-der Calder. Together they provided the main visual inspiration for a new generation of designers in search of a modern, expressive, post-Fascist, post-Modern Movement furniture aesthetic. The organic, abstract forms of the new American furniture desig-ners suggested an alternative to the rectilinear forms of Rationalist architecture and design.

The new materials and the new forms merged in the work of a number of the new architect-desig-ners in the years after 1945, in par-ticular that of Vico Magistretti, Marco Zanuso, Carlo di Carli and Osvaldo Borsani. Borsani's reclining chair, was designed for Tecno – a com-pany which emerged in the early 1950s out of a much older craft work-shop. The chair consisted of two 'wings' which moved around a metal joint thereby changing the angles of incline of both the seat and the back. It was a novel concept making use of new materials in a highly inventive way. Borsani's chair demonstrated the Italian flair for combining func-tional, material, and formal innova-tions. In many pieces by other desig-ners, foam rubber was used to cover shells made out of pressed and shaped metal. Zanuso's famous 'Lady' armchair, for example, depended entirely on foam rubber for its expres-sive curves. In 1951 Zanuso had been a co-founder of Arflex, a furniture firm which had strong links with the Pirelli company, and which was set up specifically to develop furniture using foam rubber in an imaginative and modern way.

Some Italian designers did remain

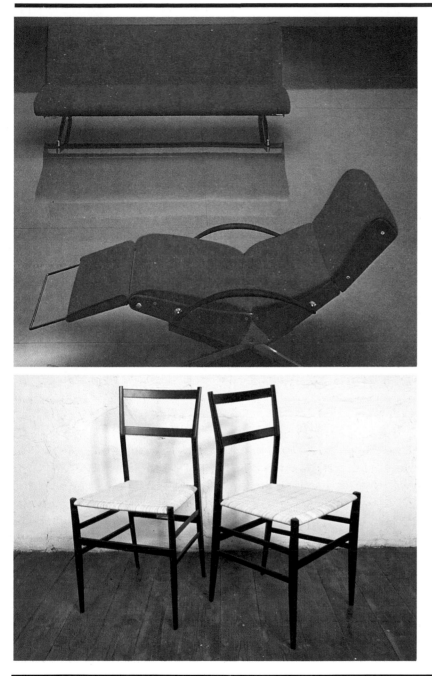

Osvaldo Borsani's 'P40' chaise longue designed for Tecno in 1954 combining a steel frame with latex foam upholstery.

committed to wood – for instance, Carlo Mollino, who developed an extraordinary range of wooden pieces in carved maple and in bent and moulded ply, which were labelled 'Turinese Baroque' and which were inspired by tree-roots and antlers' horns. Others, however, like Paolo Chessa, Paolo Buffa, Ico Parisi and Alberto Rosselli explored the possibilities of glass and plastic laminates, as well as creating new furniture items such as trolleys and mobile bars. Glass gave rise to a number of transparent pieces, while plastic laminates permitted bright colours to become yet another element in the rich language of Italian furniture. The fashions of the day were pushed further in Italy than anywhere else. The tapers of the legs were sharper, the legs themselves were more splayed and the curved forms were more exaggerated. Everything was used to achieve the greatest possible visual richness. A writer from the time described a unit production desk in

The little 'Superleggera' side chair, designed for Cassina by Gio Ponti in 1956 was inspired by the traditional fisherman's chairs produced in Chiavari in Italy.

the following terms, emphasizing its expressive qualities: *"the suavity of contour and detail overcomes the stiff budgeted look expected in modular units"*.

The material that gave Italian furniture its most distinctive style was plastic. Early experiments with plastics were made in the 1950s, particularly by the Pirelli company, which had been working on synthetic rubber since the 1930s and which sponsored much work in this area. There were also a number of new companies such as Kartell and Artemide, which, from the beginning, put a particular emphasis on plastics. It was to be a few years, however, before the research began to influence furniture design and production. The most common use of plastics in the 1950s was in the form of laminates, used to cover the flat surfaces of tables and cabinets. They provided a colourful, decorative surface in keeping with the style sought after by many Italian designers in this period.

It was the designers who were wholly responsible for the visual sophistication of the Italian pieces,

and their names were widely publicized, often indeed as the furniture's main selling point. Many of the newly-trained architects of the day saw furniture as a major symbol of Italian reconstruction and as the best means to disassociate themselves from the work of the Fascist period. They allied themselves with fine art rather than architecture, and sought to influence the mass environment in a significant way. The flexibility of the Italian furniture industry meant that what was pioneered by one firm was quickly copied by the next, and the work of the more avant-garde companies (among them Cassina, Tecno, Arflex, Artemide and Azucena) was rapidly reproduced by workshops and small factories catering for a lower level of the market. Andrea Branzi explains that *"even the smallest joiner's shop soon learnt how to work bar counters that looked like Gio Ponti's own designs; the smallest electric workshops soon learnt to make lamps that looked like Vigano's and upholsterers played on armchair models that might be reminiscent of Zanuso's"*.

It was not only the wealthy, international market, therefore, that was

Opposite: Marco Zanuso's 'Lady' chair designed for Arflex in the mid 1950s was among the first of its kind to exploit the sculptural curves made possible by foam-rubber upholstery.

affected by modern Italian design in the 1950s. In Italian cities the coffee-bar became a shrine to modernism and boasted new furniture, new plastic laminates on the counter and, most important of all, the new streamlined coffee-machines in gleaming chrome. The coffee-bar cult was imported by a number of other countries, particularly those which had a high level of Italian immigration, such as the USA and Britain, and the modern Italian furniture movement went with it, as part of the same package. It entered the popular imagination all over the world.

One area which became a special symbol of the sophistication of the Italian interior style was lighting. The fitting itself became an overtly sculptural object, forming part of the appearance of the room, while the

The 'Distex' chair designed by Gio Ponti for Cassina in 1953, an early exercise in the modern Italian style.

light emitted became an essential element in its mood. Lighting has an ambiguous relationship with furniture. It can be considered as a piece of equipment or as an intrinsic, hidden element within the room, or as a furniture object in its own right. For the Italians it performed a similar expressive function to the chairs and coffee-tables that filled their stylish interiors. At the same time, its freedom from any obviously functional use endowed it with a special sculptural role. Designers, such as the Castiglioni brothers and Gino Sarfatti, working for companies like Arteluce, Arredoluce and, a little later, Flos, concentrated on the lighting object, treating if first and foremost as a sculptural exercise. Sarfatti's designs from these years resembled the mobiles of Alexander Calder and were highly influential internationally in creating a vogue for 'lighting sculpture'. The Castiglioni brothers created a number of radical lighting designs in this period which had no visual ancestors. They described their pieces as 'techno-functionalist', because they simply applied the new material to the problem of lighting and allowed the designs that emerged to speak for themselves. 'Tubino' of 1951 was shown at the Milan Triennale of that year and consisted simply of an illuminated tube. 'Luminator', a tall, monolithic structure which shed light

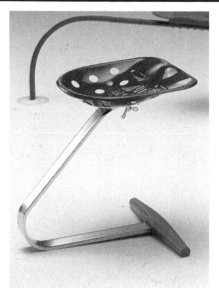

'Mezzadro' – the little tractor-seat stool designed by Achille and Pier Giacomo Castiglioni in the mid 1950s was finally manufactured by Zanotta in the early 1970s.

from its summit, was produced by Gilardi Arform in 1955. The Castiglionis also worked for the Zanotta company in this decade producing a number of highly avant-garde pieces which derived from the artist Marcel Duchamp's idea of the 'ready made'. Their best known pieces were a tractor-seat and a kneeling-stool – both of which were well in advance of their time. The Zanotta company, established by Aurelia Zanotta in 1954, produced some of the most radical Italian design of the following decade. It was an essentially small-scale firm aiming its goods at a cosmopolitan market from the very start.

The years 1958-1962 are the ones described as the 'Italian Miracle' during which period their industry expanded at an unprecedented rate and the consumer society boomed. By the early 1960s Italy had taken the lead as the major exporter of modern furniture to the rest of the world. The unique nature of its industry and the way it collaborated with architects and designers had allowed Italy to develop a sophisticated and exclusive style of furniture which yet remained visually simple and committed to new materials. By the middle of the 1960s the culture of mass consumption, which was highly developed in Northern Italy, had become intrinsically linked with the furniture movement. The pieces produced in Italy came to symbolize a modern, affluent, cosmopolitan lifestyle which was associated with the 'good life' – a concept which Ponti had outlined in his early post-war issues of *Domus*. It was an immensely seductive image and one which captured the imaginations of a large sector of the international market. 'Italian style' was in popular demand worldwide.

By the middle of the decade, however, it had its opponents. When the oil crisis began and the furniture industry went into recession in the early 1970s, its pre-eminence gradually began to fade.

10

FROM 'UTILITY' TO 'CONTEMPORARY'

THE Second World War had a tremendous effect on the production of British furniture. This was due mainly to the inevitable shortage of wood brought about by the reduction in shipping in this period. The situation was not unique to Britain, and the USA and Italy, among others, had the same difficulties. It was in Britain, however, that the Government exercised the strictest control over what little wood was available. Beyond this, it instituted a more fully state-controlled furniture production system than existed in any other country, with far-reaching effects.

The Utility scheme was introduced to ensure that enough furniture was produced during the War to meet the needs of the owners of homes destroyed by bombing and of young couples setting up home for the first time. The scheme went further than this, though. It also determined what kind of furniture should be manufactured, for what price and by whom.

A British kitchen from the 1940s furnished with Utility items.

This was the first time that a government body had been vested with enough authority to make sure that only the furniture it thought best for people was actually produced. Inevitably the 'ideal' furniture solution had to be a standardized one and it had to conform to the highest possible tenets of quality and taste – according to the criteria of those in authority. It was a unique experiment which has never been repeated since. As John Vaizey has commented, *"The War provided an opportunity for the philosophy of the economical, practical, utilitarian standards to be applied to the taste of the nation as a whole"*. Subsequent events showed, however, that while this system may work in an age of austerity, when people become more prosperous they prefer, on the whole, to make their own 'taste' mistakes.

The launch of the Utility scheme in 1942 had been preceded by timber and price controls and the encouragement of manufacturers to work only on essential items such as furniture for local authorities, the forces, and hospitals. The earlier 'Standard Emergency Furniture', initiated in 1941, was made of 80 per cent plywood, but the later Utility ranges made no use at all of this material, as from then on it was used almost exclusively in aircraft production. Wartime furniture was made of veneered hardboard instead.

Prototypes of Utility furniture items shown at an exhibition at the Board of Trade in January 1948.

The Utility advisory committee was convened in 1942, and in 1943 the Design Panel was formed, chaired by Gordon Russell. It selected the work of three men – Edwin Clinch, H.T. Cutler, and another (said to be L.T. Barnes) – to be included in the first Utility catalogue. The first range, manufactured by a list of factories selected by the Board of Trade, included a dining-table and chairs; a fireside chair; a sideboard; a kitchen cabinet; and a bedroom suite com-prising a bed, a wardrobe, a tallboy and a dressing table. In 1945 all-steel bedsteads were included as well as 'wicker' (in fact made of woven paper) furniture and in the following year the 'Chiltern' and 'Cotswold' ranges were introduced. In 1947, fol-lowing a trip Gordon Russell took to the USA to report on their furniture industry and to investigate their use of aluminium, an aluminium divan was added to the range of pieces already available.

After the end of the war the stan-dard pieces were joined by imports from Finland, Poland and Holland, but it was not until November 1948 that the Utility scheme finally granted total freedom of design once again, following the demise of furniture rationing. The lifting of restrictions was a result, primarily, of pressure from the trade, which felt the increas-ing need for diversity. The scheme was not fully played out, however, until 1952 and many manufacturers continued to make Utility pieces to Board of Trade specifications as non-Utility furniture was subject to tax.

The lasting impact of the Utility scheme was that it resuscitated the 'Arts and Crafts' principles, this time within the context of mass produc-tion. The Board of Trade talked inces-santly about such qualities as 'simplicity and refinement of design' – virtues which owed much to the writings of William Morris – and the dominance of wood, in however modified a form. In addition, the furniture's stylistic references to well-known pieces, such as the long-established Windsor chair, kept its associations with the British furniture tradition, in spite of the fact that it was manufactured by industrial means in great numbers. Utility furniture quickly penetrated the mass market, combining low price with high quality.

The essential idealism which had

motivated the Utility scheme was founded on a belief in state control over matters of quality, workmanship and design. There was a feeling among many of those involved that, for the first time, the ubiquitous 'tastelessness' of popular furniture had been replaced by standardized 'good taste'. Gordon Russell even claimed that the standards achieved by the scheme would set the tone for all post-war developments in Britain. It was to prove a rash prediction, as the post-war generation was quick to realize that it no longer wanted to be dictated to in matters of taste. The manufacturer and retailer responded immediately to a call for a renewal of novelty, variation and decoration, using every possible ploy to provide a diversity of furniture pieces for the post-war consumer.

The models presented by the USA and Scandinavia of, in the first case, the role of advanced technology and, in the second, the continued importance of tradition and human values, tended to merge stylistically on British soil in these years. Together they inspired the new furniture movement labelled 'Contemporary' which emerged in Britain in the late 1940s. They also provided a commercial model which Britain, eager to re-enter world trade, was keen to emulate.

As in the USA, the acceptance of modern furniture (alongside the continued popularity of reproduction and second-hand furniture) occurred on two levels in Britain. On the one hand it was represented by the work of a handful of progressive designers, who were sponsored by a few adventurous companies, and were committed to the concept of a new furniture. On the other, as a result of the expansion in manufacturing and retailing in these years, it also developed rapidly into a mass style eagerly adopted by the generation which was setting up home in the decade following the end of the War and which sought excitement and the new-found status attached to injecting 'modernity' into their newly-built houses.

The Government design promotion body, the Council of Industrial Design (established in 1944) was scathing about this popularized version of the Contemporary style. It labelled it 'repro-Contemporary' and dismissed it, along with the highly popular 'repro-Jacobean' pieces which were also flooding the market at this time. The campaign for 'Contemporary' was highly organized – it used books, magazines, and television programmes, all of which extolled its virtues and explained its superiority to period styles. The main impetus was the housing programmes of the period, which were centred in new towns and in estates on the edges of existing towns and cities as well as the consumer boom of these years which meant that more people than ever

before were able to purchase new pieces of furniture. The expansion of high street multiple retail outlets and the increased availability of hire purchase all contributed to the popularizing of Contemporary furniture in the years after 1945.

As in the USA the research into new materials, such as moulded plywood and the use of light metal alloys (especially aluminium and magnesium) which came out of the War, meant a whole new range of possibilities for post-war furniture. Numerous advances had been made in plywood technology during the War, as a result of work on the Mosquito airplane. Carl Jacobs' simple chair designed for Kandya was a prime example of the new possibilities offered by plywood. Moulded ply, which had been developed for the Mosquito's fuel tanks, started to be used in this period, along with bent plywood and laminated wood. Synthetic adhesives also became commonplace, making many traditional furniture joints redundant. In the immediate post-war years the chassis of countless chairs and settees were made entirely of metal, and sideboards were suspended on metal frames so as to avoid drawing on depleted timber stocks. Very often, also, materials were bonded together with the new resins to create multi-media pieces, Ernest Race, for instance, bonded a veneer of

West African mahogany to a base of laminated plastic sheeting, and Clive Latimer bonded veneers to aluminium sheets in a design for Heal's. Aluminium surfaces could be stuck on to a plastic base for table-tops and shelves. The new plastic laminates and anodized aluminium permitted a range of bright colours to enter the furniture arena, as they had in Italy, thus moving further and further away from the austerity of Utility.

The spin-offs from aircraft technology had a tremendous impact on post-war British furniture. In addition to the new woods, metals and bonding agents, sponge rubber became an increasingly popular substitute for steel springs, gradually replacing the tension springs developed by Parker-Knoll in the inter-war years. The new body line method of cushioning was the result of seating designed to enable war-time pilots to fly long distances without fatigue. A central theme of the 'Britain Can Make It' exhibition, organized by the Council of Industrial Design and held at the Victoria and Albert museum in 1946, was the appropriation of war-time technology for civilian use. One section was entitled 'From a Spitfire to a Saucepan' and was designed to explain the benefits of war-time technological achievements. While many of the room settings in the exhibition were

A Heal's bedroom suite in a room setting from the 'Britain Can Make It' exhibition held at the Victoria and Albert Museum, London, in 1946.

Below: Ernest Race's chair made of cast aluminium with rubberized cushioning and a combination cabinet, bookshelf and tray also made from aluminium shown at the 'Britain Can Make It' competition held at the Victoria and Albert Museum, London, in 1946.

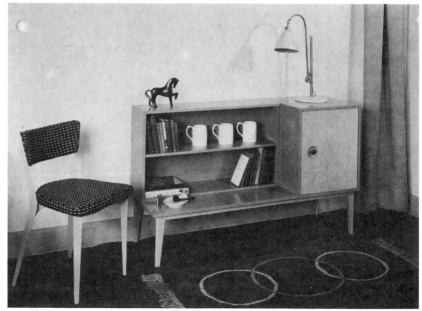

furnished with Utility pieces there were also a few post-war items such as Ernest Race's little dining-chair, the legs of which were made of T-section aluminium castings. It stood out from the pieces around it and suggested things to come. Its light form and tapered legs indicated an 18th-century influence and represented a direct challenge to the heavy 'boxiness' of so much pre-war furniture.

The other major determining factor on post-war furniture in Britain, as elsewhere, was the ever decreasing size of living spaces and the continuing need for items of furniture to be smaller, lighter and more flexible. *Ideal Home* magazine in February 1947 posed the question, 'Is a dining-room worthwhile?' and showed an example of bookshelves combined with an electric fire. Following the Scandinavian model, furniture pieces were bought, increasingly, as individual items rather than as suites, and unit furniture and interchangeability became increasingly commonplace. This tendency was apparent, however, only at the more affluent levels of the market. People with lower incomes who, for the most part, bought their furniture from high street retailers, tended to stick with the notion of suites because they followed convention and retailers needed to stock suites in order to have an impressively alluring window dis-

play. Many of the suites available in these years tended to be lighter than their predecessors, however, and the concept of the storage unit became increasingly popular as well. Selling furniture became a much more aggressive activity than before due to the fact that the market was expanding at such a phenomenal rate.

The space-saving principle, which applied to the vast majority of the population, highlighted the new light chairs with their open frames, splayed, tapered legs and winged backs. Windsor chairs made another appearance at this time also – many of them restyled by the Ercol company. They were seen as a perfect accompaniment to the Contemporary interior which, unlike the earlier 'Modernist' setting, welcomed the unison of traditional with new pieces. Ambiguous furniture items, such as room-dividers and other unit storage items (pioneered in Britain by the Gomme company which produced the range called 'G-Plan'), were highly visible in these years as was furniture which folded and packed away.

Patented originally in 1932 by an Austrian furniture manufacturer the 'nesting' principle, for instance, became widespread in the 1950s, as the pieces could be put away when they weren't in use, and countless sets of nesting tables made of bent plywood appeared on the market at this time. Stacking also became an

increasing necessity and the 'Landi' chair, originally designed by Hans Coray in 1938, with splayed legs allowing the pieces to sit on top of each other, became a model for many others to follow. The Swedish 'package' concept also entered the British scene in the mid 1950s providing, according to Gordon Logie, *"a contribution to the present-day problem of providing rapidly a large quantity of cheap and simple furniture."*

In addition to the practical problem of saving space, the Contemporary furniture aesthetic itself, which emphasized long, low lines and light colours, also helped to create an illusion of spaciousness. By the late 1940s, it was clear that the boxy Utility style was no longer desirable and a

The 'Landi' chair designed by Hans Coray in the late 1940s became a model for many of the 'stacking' experiments made at that time in response to smaller living spaces.

move had occurred in the direction of a more open, expressive idiom which incorporated pattern, colour and organic form. Plants, pictures and small decorative items became essential elements in the new humanistic interior (as they had in Sweden some years earlier). Solid furniture pieces were replaced by light, often transparent or irregularly shaped items. As in the USA, the new emphasis on wall storage cast a spotlight on the chair, which developed even more dramatically tapered legs than before, and more voluptuous upholstered curves.

The question of surface pattern on furniture inspired much discussion at this time, as there was still a feeling, in some quarters, that 'honest' construction was essential to 'good' furniture and that decoration was, therefore, highly suspect. At the upper end of the market many of the well-known designers of the day, among them Ernest Race, Robin Day, Clive Latimer and Robert Heritage, gave much thought to the vexed question of how to provide appropriate machine-made patterns for machine-made furniture. This was linked to the problem of how British furniture could retain its traditional standards yet, at the same time, supply the new market with the novelty that it so clearly wanted. In 1956 Denise Bonnett wrote that *"Contemporary design will not be able to meet this demand so long as it refuses to let any-thing appear in furniture except structure."* This, she claimed, was a lesson learnt from the 18th century, the period of inspiration for so much British furniture at this time.

The machine-made ornament that emerged in these years was characterized by the repetition of small, abstract motifs, carved in relief into the flat wooden surfaces of sideboards and a number of other furniture items, by routers. The motifs used – stars, circles, and hexagonal forms, among others – mirrored exactly those applied to the surfaces of much of the textiles, ceramics and glass in this period, thereby emphasizing the essential unity of the Contemporary interior. They were made with a jig, or template, and the repetition served to stress their mechanical origins. W.H. Russell developed a number of striking sideboards for Gordon Russell which he decorated with a regular linear pattern using a router. Robert Heritage exploited numerous techniques, including scouring with rotary wire brushes and silk screen printing, in his search for patterns to embellish the surfaces of his sideboards for G.W. Evans and Company Limited. Many of the storage items produced in this period were placed on metal or wooden plinths with splayed legs in an attempt to disguise the boxiness which was still an inevitable result of their standardized production.

While storage and carcase furniture depended upon surface ornament to provide the novelty demanded by the market, chair designs from this period exploited the structural potential of the new materials for their aesthetic variation. Both Robin Day's and Ernest Race's chairs for the 1951 Festival of Britain became highly popular examples of this particular tendency and were widely emulated. They exploited the new light style (well established by Eames across the Atlantic) which was achieved by combining moulded

Ernest Race's 'Antelope' chair in steel and moulded plywood of 1951 (right) and steel rocking chair of the same year (left).

The steel and plastic 'Springbok' chair designed by Ernest Race, was a ubiquitous feature of the 1951 Festival of Britain.

plywood with steel rod. (With Clive Latimer, Day, in fact, beat Eames to first place in a competition at the Museum of Modern Art in New York in 1949.) The organic shapes of the '51 chairs were influenced as much by the human form, and by the curves of contemporary sculpture, as they were by new technology. Contemporary critics stressed their combined qualities of strength, lightness and comfort. A writer in a guide to young marrieds explained that *"Contemporary chairs with slender legs, exposed frames and light latex upholstery look rather less comfortable and a great deal less solid than the traditional stuffed variety. But looks are no guide to chair comfort."*

In Britain, the 1950s saw a number of new developments in the area of domestic furniture, notable among them the advent of the named designer, who became a mass media hero. Articles were written about these designers in the press. In one *Ideal Home Yearbook*, for instance, there was a piece entitled 'At Home with the Days', which looked at the exciting way in which Robin Day and his wife Lucienne had furnished their domestic interiors. Besides this, huge efforts were made by a number of small pioneering companies, among them Hille, Race, Kandya, Heal's, Gomme, Archie Shine, Ercol, H.K. Furniture and Gordon Russell Limited, to commit themselves totally to modern furniture production.

The other major achievement of these years was the rapidly growing interest of the general British public in modern furniture. One of the factors in this was the growing popularity of the 'Do-It-Yourself' movement, imported initially from the USA. People were encouraged to make their own bookshelves, lamps, plant-stands, coffee-tables, trolleys and even cocktail bars – in, of course, the Contemporary style, or as near as they could get to it. This was made easier by the wide availability of machine-processed wood and the new glues. Equally important was the increasing affluence of the average British family in these years and its eagerness to reject war-time austerity once and for

A room divider from the 1950s designed by Robin Day.

all, and to move wholesale into a bright new modern age. The furniture now being produced proposed a lifestyle which had nothing in common with the pre-war way of life, and many people who had not bought new furniture before went to their local high street retailer in search of

sofas, easy chairs and room dividers with which to create their own Contemporary interiors. Ernest Race observed this phenomenon and commented at the time that, *"perhaps the*

Left: A sideboard by Robert Heritage from the mid 1950s showing repeated, machine-made surface pattern created with a router.

Bottom left: The British show flat at the exhibition held in Hälsingborg in Sweden in 1955 which contains a coffee-table and occasional chair designed by Robin Day; a shelf and storage unit by Conran Furniture; and a settee and chair designed by Ward and Austin.

Below: The interior of a business man's flat in the 'contemporary' style designed by A. V. Pilley and illustrated in Noel Carrington's Colour and Pattern in the Home *of 1954.*

most significant development of the last year has come not so much from the manufacturers, retailers and designers, but from the public itself", but he went on to lament the appearance of the 'watered-down' Contemporary furniture available on the high street. Gordon Russell also regretted deeply that such *"features as tapered legs will be overplayed"*: The gap between the new furniture of these years which had Council of Industrial Design approval, and the more popular designs, was clearly defined. This popular appropriation of modern furniture did not mean, however, that traditional furniture was no longer being bought. In 1952 Russell pointed out that there were six types of furniture on sale in Britain: *"antiques, second-hand, reproduction antiques, pure commercial style, contemporary and imitations of contemporary."* Only the last two fell into the 'modern' category.

What was abundantly clear was that the control exerted by the wartime Utility scheme had given way to a stylistic free-for-all and that more people than ever before were participating in it.

The exuberance of this period was short-lived, however. It became apparent by the end of the decade that, the Council of Industrial Design (fearing a revival of the visual anarchy of the Victorian period), was trying hard to reassert the importance of visual

A window seat and cocktail trolley from the early 1950s designed by Dennis Lennon and illustrated in Noel Carrington's book Colour and Pattern in the Home *of 1954.*

restraint in modern furniture. One furniture item to be given a Council award in the late 1950s was a wooden sideboard, designed by Robert Heritage for Archie Shine. It was rectilinear in form, and had a caption describing its 'straightforward functional simplicity, well suited to modern life'. Another award winner was a settee-bed, designed by Robin Day Hille, which also had a definite squareness of form. This marked return to the 'box' not only had the approval of the Co.I.D., but was also economic to produce. It marked a very noticable change from the early decade when pattern and verve had been so much in evidence.

PART FOUR

FURNITURE FOR THE CONSUMER SOCIETY (1961-1985)

WHILE the immediate post-war years can be seen, in many ways, as the 'heroic' period of modern domestic furniture (the time when it broke away from architecture and when an international modern style was formed), the years after 1960 were ones of consolidation followed by reaction. Mainstream modern furniture design became, in this later period, more static than before, adopting an image which suggested international affluence. It linked itself increasingly with 'Italian Chic' rather than with 'Scandinavian Modern', and, instead of seeking after democratic idealism, it became part of world trade and metropolitan high style.

The bulk of furniture production in these years reflected the increasing size and standardization of the industry in a number of countries, including Austria, Holland, France and Britain. The period was characterized by a general expansion through the boom years of the 1960s, followed by a sharp drop in sales, experienced internationally, when the recession of the 1970s took a hold. The lack of flexibility that could be achieved with mass production became an increasing problem to a large sector of the international furniture industry as time progressed. As a result, the USA lost its dominance, while Italy and Scandinavia fared better.

Technologically the era was the one in which plastics finally came into their own. Their hey-day was in the 1960s, mainly as a result of the advances made by the Italians, but the oil crisis of the early 1970s quickly rendered plastic too expensive, and it was forced to give way to more traditional materials, particularly wood.

As a reaction to the way mainstream furniture was becoming the province of an international wealthy middle-class, another development began to take place. Initiating in Great Britain, a young, stylish throwaway style of furniture was designed, to suit the new 'Pop' environment. A number of young furniture designers from different countries evolved this type of expendable furniture, thereby undermining the status quo which depended increasingly, on the twin concepts of luxury and durability. These designers tended, on the whole, to work outside the confines of the mass production industry and to challenge its commercial assumptions. The Pop furniture movement, which grew out of these rebellious gestures, reached its high point in Italy, where it first made a brief appearance in the 1960s, and then re-emerged fully-fledged, in the late 1970s and early 1980s. Finland also experimented with Pop furniture, combining it with the colours and forms made possible by the use of plastics.

In general, however, the period from the late 1960s onwards was characterized less by technological innovations that by the way furniture sought to conform with cultural change. It aligned itself with a number of cultural movements, from the Crafts Revival, to the nostalgia boom, to the ecology movement, to Post-Modernism, in a series of attempts to reach new markets and to justify its role in the mass environment. By the late 1970s cultural pluralism had become an essential element within the furniture production. It was expressed in a range of alternative styles, available internationally to a variety of markets and suggesting many alternative lifestyles.

Two examples from Robert Venturi's range of bent plywood chairs designed for Knoll International in 1984. On the left is the Art Deco version and on the right, his interpretation of a Sheraton chair – they share the same profile.

11

THE CHALLENGE
OF
POP CULTURE

A number of changes took place in Britain in the years after 1960 which dramatically altered the relationship between mass produced furniture and the public. 1957 marked, according to the social historian Arthur Marwick, the advent of the consumer society in Britain and, from that moment onwards, more people than ever before began to take part in the adventure of buying new furniture. They had more money in their pockets and credit was widely available. In a rush to meet the needs of this swelling market, furniture manufacturers stepped up their production and expanded in size. This continued through the 1960s, and then reached a crisis in the early 1970s when the recession began to be felt. By going in for volume production, the manufacturers had sacrificed their flexibility and could no longer meet the needs of varied markets, as they had done so effectively back in the 1930s.

The move towards larger production units was constant during the 1950s and 1960s. In 1950 there had been 2824 firms manufacturing furniture in Britain. By 1958 this number had dropped to 1714, but they were larger and more profitable than the earlier ones. This change in the industry led to a greater concentration on low- and medium-priced products and, as a result, a predominantly conservative attitude towards design. Suites of furnitue persisted, as styles continued to depend upon Scandinavian models. Imports also expanded in these years, mainly from Scandinavia, Germany and Eastern Europe, but exports dropped sharply and by the early 1970s the industry was in trouble.

The general picture of the British furniture industry in the 1960s emphasized standardization, rationalization and automation. The Lebus company, for instance, rationalized its production very radically in 1968, reducing the number of its lines and cutting down on manual labour. To cut costs, much whitewood furniture was imported from abroad and finished in British factories. A large amount of built-in and fitted furniture started to come off the production lines, when solid particle or chipboard came to the fore as a cheap substitute for ply-wood. The 'boxy' look of much of the furniture of the 1960s was a direct result of the mass produced veneered chipboard carcases for storage furniture, which could be knocked flat for transporting and storage. Traditional objects such as wardrobes, sideboards, and chests of drawers took longer to disappear in Britain, however, than in Scandinavia and Germany where more research and innovatory work was undertaken.

Increasingly, chip-board carcase furniture for kitchens, living-rooms dining-rooms and bedrooms was sold in its flat state, for the purchaser to construct himself. The Do-It-Yourself movement took an even stronger hold in these years and many manufacturers sold their furniture in kits, thereby reducing costs in warehousing, display and transport. This tendency continued through the 1960s and into the 1970s and 1980s bringing with it radical implications for the retailing of mass-produced furniture.

The increased availability of furniture for the mass market was, in fact, made possible by changes in the way furniture was marketed in Britain after the War. With the advent of Terence Conran's Habitat store on the Fulham Road in 1964, and the chain that developed from it, the 1960s witnessed a significant change in the way that furniture was sold on the high street. Conran opened his first shop following his failure to sell the furniture he had designed and made himself through existing retail outlets. At this time the only outlets for furniture were either the department store (which supplied a predominantly middle class market with its 'quality' reproduction and Contemporary pieces) or the high street multiple stores which catered for mass taste. By the end of the 1950s it had become apparent that there was a huge discrepancy in the type, style and quality of furniture that was being offered to different social groups on Britain. While the predominantly London-based department stores such as Harrods, Whiteleys,

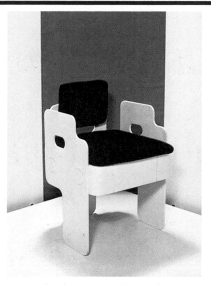

Max Clendenning's plywood-framed chair from the 'Maxima' range designed for Race Furniture Limited in 1966.

Peter Jones and Storys maintained the standards of quality that they had established back in the 19th century, the high street depended on furniture which combined immediate visual impact with low price. In his book *The Uses of Literacy*, written in the late 1950s, Richard Hoggart described these furniture shops in some detail pinpointing them as one of the main purveyors of working-class taste: *"At first glance these are surely the most hideously tasteless of all modern shops. Every known value in decoration has been disregarded: there is no evident design or pattern; the colours fight with one another;*

anything new is thrown in simply because it is new."

Much of the furniture for sale, from the late 1950s through into the 1960s in these shops, had a high gloss finish and used decorative veneers. It was a style which was as at home on radiograms, TV consoles and cocktail cabinets as on more conventional items such as sideboards and dining-suites. The high street multiple store of the 1950s and 1960s, which directed its wares at the new furniture consumer, was often an expanded version of the smaller furniture shop of yesteryear. Many, such as John Perrings and Times Furnishings, had started off as modest, family-based furniture shops established during the first wave of mass consumption at the end of the 19th century. It was in 1894 for instance that John Jacobs opened his first store in London. By 1957 Times Furnishings had expanded into 45 branches throughout England. The shop's commitment both to hire purchase and to the 'ordinary' consumer sowed the seeds for its later success. It remained a family firm right up until 1968 when it merged with a large marketing organization.

Through the 1950s and 1960s Times Furnishings provided 'modern' furniture for the mass market. It dealt with many of the well known mass furniture manufacturers of the day — among them Beautility, Wrighton, Sleepeezee, Cintique, Nathan,

Parker-Knoll, Ercol, Gomme and Stag – all of which were committed to volume-produced, reasonably priced pieces which reflected furniture trends in the more expensive, international market. In 1957, for instance, the Beautility company was producing suites called 'Nordic' and 'Milan', in recognition of the fashion for Scandinavian and Italian furniture at that time. Both were sold through the Times stores. Developments in communications and the mass media were so rapid at this time that international furniture styles were immediately available to a wide sector of the market.

The major 'cultural revolution' that occurred in the 1960s was the burgeoning of a wealthy youth market. This coincided with Terence Conran's project to revolutionize the way that furniture was sold by providing 'packaged good taste' for a young market which wanted to buy a complete lifestyle rather than just a suite of furniture. Habitat was the 'boutique' of the furniture retailers offering the same instant, yet carefully pre-selected, taste values that Mary Quant and John Stephens were marketing through their fashion shops. In 1967 Habitat expanded by adding a Manchester branch to its two existing London stores and from there it developed into the international multiple that it is today.

Inevitably, many of the more progressive furniture experiments of the 1960s could only be directed initially at a fairly exclusive audience, but some of them filtered into the more fashion-conscious shops which catered for a young market, among them The Merchant Chandler in the Fulham Road, Goods and Chattels in Neal Street, Gear in Carnaby Street, and Habitat. Many of them sold new pieces of furniture alongside second-hand military uniforms and Union Jack tea-towels. The young 'Pop' market purchased all its lifestyle accompaniments in one place and furniture for the young market was viewed in ephemeral light as a fashion item or a Pop poster.

Gradually a number of young designers began to integrate the new values into their work and, by the middle of the decade, it had become possible to speak of a Pop furniture movement which existed alongside music, fashion and the other expendable items of the time. Its impact on the mass market was fairly minimal in Britain, but it became, nonetheless, one of the inspiring forces behind the international 'post-modern' furniture movement. A growing dissatisfaction developed with the 'lasting' values of the architectural and design Modern movement, which had set out to create, among other things, the 'universal, styleless chair'. In response to this changing mood, as well as to the ever-diminishing size of many homes, furniture experiments began to emphasize flexibility and portability again. A number of pieces of furniture appeared which came apart or collapsed or could be thrown away and replaced. They were lightly decorative and, in the words of Reyner Banham, worked on the basis of a "massive initial impact, but small sustaining power".

In 1965 the British graphic designer Michael Wolff wrote, in the *Journal of the Society of Industrial Artists* that, *"It will be a great day when furniture and cutlery designs (to name but two) swing like the Supremes"* thereby heralding the new movement. This followed closely on the heels of an article in the *Sunday Times Supplement* of the previous year which had prophesied that, *"1964 will be the year we can stop persuading ourselves that we're a nation that 'buys to last'…. this year there will be more attractive, relatively inexpensive furniture which faces its transitory nature and makes the most of it"*.

It was in 1965 that Nicholas Frewing's chair, which came completely apart, was designed for Race. On one level, it simply carried on the knock-down principle that the Scandinavians had pioneered some years earlier. It also served, however, to provide an alternative to the much more 'permanent' Modern chair of the inter-war years. Knock-down was

The 'Flexible' easy chair designed by Nicholas Frewing for Race Furniture Limited in 1966 constructed on the 'knock-down' principle for easy storage and distribution.

quickly joined by the concept of 'throw-away' furniture which was much more explicit in its intentions and could be literally discarded when it had outlived its usefulness; much of it was, in fact, made either of paperboard or of thin plywood. Peter Murdoch's so-called 'paper' chair, for example, was manufactured by Perspective Designs in 1965. Made of paperboard, it was decorated with brightly coloured dots and covered with a coating of washable polythene which made it fairly tough. The material consisted of five laminations from three different papers and the

design was cut from a flat sheet of the board and folded to form the shape of a tub chair: it could be bought flat and assembled at home. The paper chair was the ultimate Pop object – both literally and symbolically – and although it never went beyond small-scale production it was widely copied. Max Clendenning's 'Jigsaw' furniture of the same year, which was cut out of thin sheets of ply was more hard wearing than the paper chairs but, with its bright painted surfaces, it expressed the same spirit of fun and youthfulness. Bernard Holdaway's plywood pieces for Hull Traders were also inspired by the same ethos, as was Martin Sylvester's 'Studio' range, made of birch laminate but stained in bright Pop colours. Most of these knock-down pieces were sold through mail order, thereby by-passing the retailer altogether.

The final manifestation of expendability in furniture came with the appearance of 'blow-up' items which

could simply be deflated when they weren't needed. Here Italy led the way with Zanotta's famous 'Blow' chair, but it was quickly followed in Britain by a chair by Arthur Quarmby; a version by Conran Associates for Habitat; and another by Roger Dean for Hille which was covered in red fun fur but which never got beyond the early production stages. The blow-up principle, (which had been originally developed to enable people to read the newspaper in the swimming pool) became ubiquitous in the Pop environment. It was made possible by the discovery of seam-welded PVC. Zanotta advertised its chair as *"not only to have in the house but to take into the country and to sail on the sea"*, while Conran described his blow-up as a *"perfect picnic chair."*

Furniture from this period

A sitting room designed by Max Clendenning in 1965.

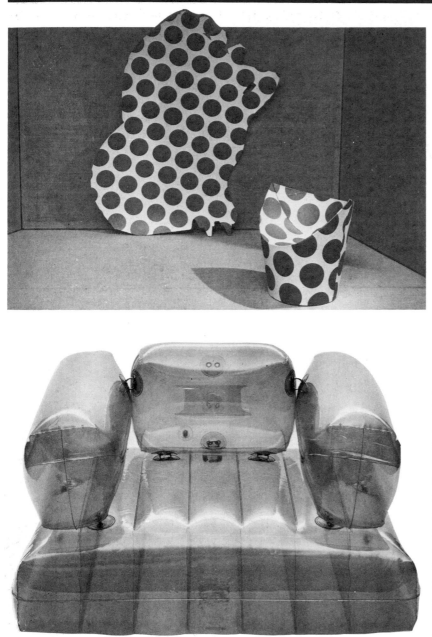

A child's chair, made of polyethylene-coated laminated paperboard designed by Peter Murdoch in 1964 and manufactured originally in the USA.

became increasingly flexible and portable, rejecting the imagery of static, status-ridden objects. This reflected the desire for social mobility which was a characteristic of the 1960s and which motivated a number of designers to search for new directions in domestic furniture. The breakdown of class barriers turned out, of course, to be just one of the many myths of that decade, and much of the experimental furniture vanished almost as soon as it appeared. The ultimate statement of their idea 'furniture as services rather than status symbol' came, in Britain, through the work of the architectural group, Archigram. In an exhibition at Woollands in the middle of the decade, this group went so far as to propose an environment which contained no conventional items of furniture whatsoever. Seating was provided by a soft, heated floor in the living-room area and the interior also contained a C-shaped couch or 'snug' sunk into the floor and a dining-table which pulled out from under the floor. Archigram's project represented an extreme ver-

An inflatable PVC chair designed by Quasar Khanh in 1967.

sion of the 'landscape' furniture idea which was illustrated in numerous glossy magazines in the 1960s. It usually consisted of undulating 'free-form' furniture pieces which were no more than lumps of polyurethane foam upholstered and placed casually in an interior so that people could lounge freely among them. While the concept was experimented with in Britain to a certain extent, it was much more popular on the Continent, particularly in Germany, France and Holland.

Above: Eero Aarnio's moulded glass-fibre 'Pastilli' chair designed for Asko in 1968.

Below: The 'Globe' chair, designed by Eero Aarnio for Asko in 1968, quickly became a major example of 'Pop' furniture in that decade.

The OMK Company's black leather and tubular steel furniture from the early 1970s recalling the geometrical austerity of early Modern Movement pieces.

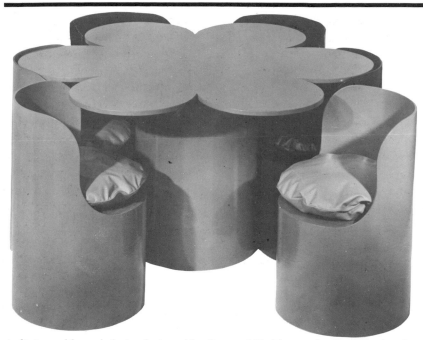

A dining table and chairs designed by Bernard Holdaway for Hull Traders in 1966, made of compressed paper tubes and chipboard and available in a range of bright colours.

The gap between Pop and the mass market shrunk a little in Britain in the 1960s, but it proved to be only a fairly minor and, indeed, temporary rapprochement. As Margaret Duckett explained, *"the colourful visual revolution has only touched the surface of the massive teak mausoleum"* and the lasting style of that decade remained the geometric one, which had replaced the splayed legs and extravagances of the 1950s. The reasons, as Nigel Walters explained in 1961, were inevitably linked to economics. *"With relatively stable market prices and constantly rising labour costs, manufacturers are more willing than ever before to accept simple straightforward designs – perpendicular legs, large plain surfaces and extruded handles are accepted with enthusiasm, where a few years ago they would not have been entertained."* The influence of Scandinavia was still apparent in the wooden-framed sofas, dining-tables and chairs that filled the high streets, and, in seating, polyurethane foam was widely used replacing the metal springs and the foam rubber of recent years. In 1968 José Manser explained that she felt the Pop revolution had failed because, *"furnishing a home represents the feathering of the nest which will always, for emotional reasons, incline towards the permanent to the extent that when the nest becomes impermanent or expendable... the transportable feathering will remain the constant factor."*

Some innovative furniture also emerged in this period, based on the achievements of the previous decade, among them pieces by Heritage for Race, and by Robin Day and Alan Turville for Hille: Days' polypropylene stacking chair, for instance, became a leader in its field. As in the 1950s, the most notable developments were sponsored by small companies but now their most interesting pieces were directed at the contract rather than the domestic market.

By the late 1960s, the industry had ceased to be able to rely on the same captive market that had supported it ten years earlier and the impact of the recession was beginning to be felt. Since the early post-war years, British industry had become either more giant-like and automated, or smaller and more design-conscious. All the large firms followed the lead of their smaller colleagues where innovative design was concerned, providing cheaper, watered-down versions for the mass market. The large companies were generally still geared to wood as a basic material but, by the end of the decade, were becoming aware of the need to move into plastics – a move which proved short-lived because of the oil crisis in the early 1970s. The British furniture industry also demonstrated, at this time, a great resistance to marketing and it was Margaret Duckett who pointed out that British manufacturers were unprepared to launch new designs purely to attract publicity. (She cited, in sharp contrast, the example of the Finnish firm Asko which had commissioned Eero Aarnio's 'Globe' chair as a publicity stunt.) The shortsightedness of the British industry did not promise it a very rosy future. By 1970 sales were well down compared to the previous year and it was clear that the boom was drawing to an end. Compared with the Germans and the French, the British public spent less money on furniture, one reason for which was undoubtedly the prolific secondhand market.

One of the most significant cultural developments of the late 1960s in Britain was the growing interest in stylistic revivalism and an increasing feeling of nostalgia for the past. In addition to rising costs, this encouraged the boom in the popularity of second-hand furniture. Back in the mid 1960s Habitat's interior style had been based on a mixture of old and new and, at the same time, shops like Gear of Carnaby Street had supplied old pine chests revamped with psychadelic colours and patterns. It wasn't long before a Victorian revival was in full swing. This was partly explained by the cessation of building in this period, and the subsequent interest in renovating older houses, but it was also part of a general interest in the past, rather than the future, which accompanied the economic recession of these years.

It was an interest which became entrenched as the recession got under way in the early 1970s by which time the style of the 1920s and 1930s had replaced the Victorian period as the subject of a tremendous period revival. Second-hand furniture from those decades was purchased voraciously by young consumers and many new designs were borrowed from them. In addition to the popular, large stuffed sofas, a range of more 'Modernist' pieces in tubular steel and black leather also emerged, produced by a number of small progressive companies including Zeev Aram and Associates; OMK; Plush Kicker; and Minale Tattersfield, all of who joined the 'Neo-Bauhaus' bandwagon of those years. The general nostalgia of the time also affected the manufacturing process, and the early 1970s saw the beginnings of an interest in the work of the designer-craftsman. This was a theme which grew in significance as the 1970s progressed.

The atmosphere in British furniture in the early 1970s was a very different one from that of ten years earlier. In a catalogue to an exhibition held at the Victoria and Albert Museum, Margaret Timmers summed up the difference, *"Following the febrile creative excitement of the 1960s, the early years of the 1970s seemed marked by a quieter mood of assimilation and consolidation"*. The furniture industry was in recession and the spread of 'good taste' to the mass market, pioneered by the 1960s method of retailing, had not really amounted to anything. Habitat had moved into the high street, and became just another chain store, more and more people bought their furniture from the giant warehouses which appeared on the edges of towns and which catered for every stylistic preference, albeit in cheap copies of the originals. The experiments with new forms and materials that had looked so exciting in 1967 had failed to transform the essential conservatism of the British furniture trade and of the majority of the public.

In the early 1970s all eyes were still focused on Italy which, with its predominantly small-scale, flexible furniture industry, and its high design profile was able to adapt to changing circumstances in a way British industry had become less and less able to do.

12

FROM CONSPICUOUS CONSUMPTION TO 'ANTI-FURNITURE'

THE years after 1960 saw a rapid boom in the wealth of certain sectors of Italian society, and in the international success of the Italian furniture industry. Almost overnight Italy had replaced Scandinavia as the home of good modern furniture, and Italian designers hit the headlines in the design press as the heroes of the new furniture movement.

Italian furniture did not set out to fulfil the democratic ideal so fundamental to the work of the Nordic countries. Instead Italy developed a much more sumptuous, fine-art oriented movement which appealed to the style-conscious rather than the socially aware. Making skilled use of the new materials, and helped by the backing of many new companies, Italian designers set out to evolve an elegant modern furniture image which concentrated on quality rather than quantity. Unlike the Scandinavians, for whom tradition and craftsmanship always remained essential, the Italians were swift to sever all links with the past.

The 1960s was the decade in which plastics finally came into their own, and this was as apparent in furniture as in other things. The worry that the public might be less ready to accept a new material for a traditional item like a chair than they would for, say, a telephone or a radio, did not daunt the Italians. By the early 1960s they had gone further than any other nation in evolving production techniques and a new image for plastic furniture.

The first major sortie into plastic furniture was made, however, in the USA by Charles Eames with his entry for the 1948 Low-Cost Furniture competition held by the Museum of Modern Art in New York. It was Eames who had evolved the idea of a one-piece moulded plastic shell used as a chair seat (his DAR chair was made of glass fibre reinforced plastic). While Eames' design was available only in drab colours (off-white, light grey and brown) and had a steel-rod base, Saarinen took the idea one step further in his 1956 'Tulip' chair for Knoll (see illustration on p.57), which had an aluminium base covered with white nylon making it look like part of the same structure. In 1960 the Dane, Verner Panton, made the first one-piece moulded plastic chair designed with a cantilevered construction (see illustration on p.53).

The Italian foray into plastic furniture had no connection with this pioneering work, however. It emerged, instead, from the researches of individuals working within a few forward-looking Italian manufacturing companies. One such firm was Kartell, formed in 1949 by its subsequent managing director, Giulio Castelli. The first object Kartell manufactured was a car ski-rack which had been developed by a Pirelli engineer and the architect-designer

Roberto Menghi. Made of rubber and elastic straps this was not a plastic product but it led the way forwards to a range of car accessories which were.

In 1953 Kartell began the mass production of a range of small, plastic household objects, ranging from dustpans to lemon squeezers, nearly all of which were designed by Gino Colombini, a designer who had worked previously in Franco Albini's studio. From the beginning, research into plastics technology and concern for aesthetic design went hand in hand. Kartell designs stressed the fact that plastics were legitimate, modern and symbolic of the new, mechanized society. It was in 1963 that the company entered the furnishings business and its first product was a small, all plastic, stackable child's chair designed by the architect-designer Marco Zanuso, who had been closely involved with the experiments in foam rubber undertaken by the Arflex company back in the 1950s. (Arflex was, in fact, founded by the same Pirelli engineer who had worked on Kartell's ski-rack.)

Zanuso's chair, which was made of injection moulded high density polythene (the next plastic after fibreglass to be used in furniture) demonstrated the fusion of his interest in new forms with his respect for technology. The legs were moulded separately and the backs

Left: Mario Bellini's luxurious leather armchair for Cassina from 1973 recalls the traditional leather club armchair while remaining totally modern in style.

Below: In this interior the buttonless version of the Scarpa's 'Coronado' suite for B and B Italia provides the image of luxury and sophistication expected from mainstream Italian furniture at this time.

and seats were striated to maximize the chair's flexibility, because of the essential rigidity of the material. It marked a major breakthrough for Italian furniture design and inspired a number of other companies to move into the same area of research.

Artemide, for instance, enlisted the assistance of Vico Magistretti in the development of a dining-set made entirely of plastic. Research began in the early 1960s but the results were not available until the middle of the decade. When they finally appeared, however, the 'Selene' chair, and its accompanying table, 'Studio 80', were quickly adopted in countless smart interiors – both domestic and otherwise. Although initially made in glass fibre reinforced plastic, this was later replaced by ABS plastic. The chair was fabricated in one piece out of a sheet of ABS and the subtle curves of its planes and the smooth radii of its bends made it one of the most sophisticated pieces of plastic furniture to come out of Italy in this period. The first models were available only in bright apple green but it could be bought later also in black, white, red and orange.

Among the other pieces of Italian plastic furniture manufactured in the 1960s were some shelves, trolleys and small storage stystems designed by Anna Castelli Ferrieri for Kartell and a Joe Colombo chair produced by the same company – the first ever one-piece injection moulded chair. With such examples, Italy succeeded in turning plastic from a cheap substitute material for furniture into an extremely elegant one, in a way that inspired countless similar experiments in other countries.

While Kartell, Artemide and a few other manufacturers excelled in the design and production of 'hard' plastic furniture, the Zanotta company specialized, at this time, in developing techniques for making and using polyurethane foam. In 1967 it launched 'Throwaway', a sofa designed by Willie Landels which was the first of its kind to be made entirely of foam, with no wooden or metal

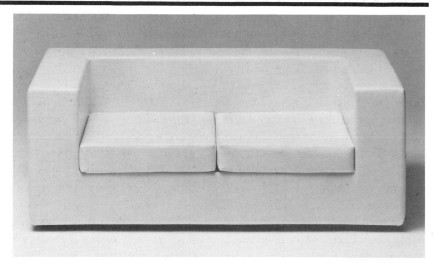

'Throwaway' – a sofa designed by Willie Landels for Zanotta in 1967.

structure to support it.

For Italy, plastics served as a means of developing mass-produced, elegant furniture pieces which carried that country's style into cosmopolitan centres all over the world. It remained a strong element within the Italian design movement as a whole up until the early 1970s when the energy crisis finally made it uneconomical to continue to use plastics.

The rise of plastic furniture was not, however, the only Italian success story of the 1960s. A great deal of their modern furniture began to exploit such luxurious materials as marble, black leather, smoked glass and chrome, and it is this exclusive furniture style for which Italy has become best known since the War. New companies, such as B and B

Italia, Saporiti, Sormani, and a host of others grew up in the 1960s, with the close co-operation of the well-known designers of the day. Increasingly Italian furniture meant expensive furniture and, by the end of the decade, it had succeeded in dominating the international market. Padded upholstered forms replaced the light, open-structured Scandinavian pieces and, instead of creating small items for small homes, the Italian designers assumed that only people with ample space could afford modern furniture. Mainstream Italian furniture from this period is well represented by Mario Bellini's leather and marble pieces for Cassina, and by items such as 'Coronada' designed by Tobia Scarpa for B and B Italia. Leather-padded seats and other luxury materials created an image of eminently 'bourgeois' furniture which replaced their previous obsession with antiques and reproduction period furniture. Often, however, both types of furniture were featured alongside one another in the same setting in the glossy Italian magazines of the period. The modern designs were, by implication, the new 'classics'. Italian furniture combined a sense of comfort with quality and modernity, communicated through the materials used, a high degree of workmanship, and an attention to visual detail. By the early 1970s this exclusive image had established a model which was emulated internationally. The Italian items themselves remained highly elitist, reserved for a wealthy market which wanted to invest in 'good taste'. The style did, however, filter into popular imagination through the home pages of journals, and by being included in many advertisements of the time, and in countless Italian 'B' movies. In cheaper forms the style penetrated the mass market all over the world.

Within Italy itself, however, there were signs that a number of architects and designers were beginning by the mid 1960s to resent the way in which their skills had been so easily bought by the manufacturing industry. They started to seek ways out of what they saw as the cul-de-sac of a modern furniture movement based on conspicu-

ous consumption. This 'crisis of conscience' began as a local affair, mainly in Florence, but by the end of the 1970s and the beginning of the 1980s, it had become international.

The Italian 'counter-design' movement, as it came to be called, took its impetus from the ideas and images of the British Pop movement and looked to the comic-book images of future cities proposed by the Archigram group. A number of Florence-based architectural teams, among them Archizoom, Superstudio, Gruppo Strum and others, experimented with similar visions of the future environment.

No single figure was more influential in providing the philosophical bases for this movement than the Italian architect-designer, Ettore Sottsass, based in Milan. In the mid 1960s he had produced two series of prototype furniture pieces for the Poltronova company which were inspired by the images of the Pop artists in Britain and the USA. The first set included desks which looked like bank safes and cabinets which were reminiscent of traffic lights, while the second range had more in common with young high street fashions than with conventional furniture. All the pieces could be used, however, as traditional items, whether desks or wardrobes. While these radical gestures were as far removed from the ordinary man in the street as the work of Rietveld and Mies van der Rohe had been 40 years

Superstudio's plastic laminate table designed in 1971 and manufactured by Zanotta which sets out to create a 'neutral' surface like that on the page of an exercise book.

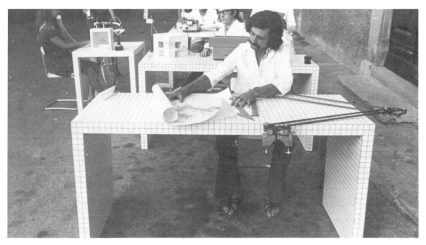

An interior setting from the late 1960s containing Tobia and Afra Scarpa's leather 'Coronado' suite designed for B and B Italia.

level, this was a playful exercise, in keeping with the spirit of the fun-loving '60s, on another it was a serious attack on the traditional notions of furniture as craftsmanship, as social status and as static monuments. The 12 million expanded polystyrene granules that are said to fill the 'Sacco' made it a formless, flexible, object – a tribute to the ethic of Pop. Numerous variations on a theme followed in the wake of Zanotta's experiment, among them Gaetano Pesce's 'Up' chair for B and B Italia. Made of polyurethane foam, the chair was compressed and packed in a flat box but, when unsealed, the foam expanded back to its original form. Pesce described it himself, using true Pop terminology, *"It loves everything which is mobile, endless, non-repeatable, inconstant, not blocked,*

The 'Sacco' designed by Gatti, Paolini and Teodora for Zanotta – it is filled with thousands of granules made of expanded polystyrene.

earlier, their message did likewise filter through, eventually, into the mass environment. Sottsass's furniture was a kind of metaphor for the rejection of the modernist idea that furniture design is simply the result of its process of manufacture. He proposed, instead, that furniture should ally itself symbolically with the mass environment of which, ultimately, it is destined to become a part.

The counter-design, or 'anti-furniture' movement also went into mass-production in Italy to a limited extent. In this context the Zanotta company played an important part. It had been quick, back in the 1950s, to

use designers, and in the mid 1960s it continued to link itself with the activities of the avant-garde, first with the 'Blow' chair and soon afterwards with the 'Sacco' which became the model for the 'bean bag' chair of the late 1960s – familiar internationally in children's bedrooms and young peoples' living rooms. According to popular myth the 'Sacco' seat emerged first as an accident, when polystyrene off-cuts were thrown into a bag at the end of the production line. It became the first popular exponent of the idea that furniture should not remain static but should move with the human body. While, on one

Gaetano Pesce's 'Up' chair made of polyurethane foam manufactured by C and B Italia in 1969.

diverse, relative, improbable, not programmed, unforeseen, not desired, not chosen, incoherent, discontinued, new......"

By the early 1970s the first phase of Italian anti-furniture had largely faded from view. In a new attack on élitism, the designers abandoned the object altogether and instead used manifestoes, exhibitions, and 'happenings' as means of stating their case and of challenging the status quo. A large exhibition of Italian furniture held in New York in 1973, called *The New Domestic Landscape*, represented the work of the radical designers alongside the luxurious leather sofas which continued to pour out of the furniture workshops and factories. The exhibition organizer isolated three directions in Italian furniture at that time labelling them, 'conformist, reformist and the furniture of contestation'. At that point, the final category seemed to have almost played itself out, but, by the end of the decade, it was to find renewed energies and to penetrate the mass market much more forcibly.

The late 1960s and early 1970s saw in Italy, as elsewhere, a recession in the furniture industry. The optimistic vision, formed several years earlier, of people sitting in cheap, brightly-coloured plastic furniture in capsule kitchens, sunken dining-rooms, and plastic-moulded micro-environments, had been a short-lived pipe dream. Traditional values and 'status' materials gradually reasserted themselves and the technological revolution seemed to have come to an abrupt end. The final death throes of the old optimism were seen at the 1973 New York exhibition, but by then 'classless' plastic furniture and flexible, radical anti-furniture were already on the way out. In the recession of the early 1970s, neo-conservatism dominated high-class furniture. It was an idiom originally formulated in Italy, but it was widely aped, usually with inferior materials and craftsmanship. It entered the public's imagination through glossy magazines, and by the end of the decade furniture was seen, once again, as a rich man's privilege.

13

FURNITURE IN THE AGE OF PLURALISM

IN the years after 1973 the practical function of furniture became less significant than the part it played in creating lifestyles. This completely altered the major motivation for change in furniture design.

The reason for this shift of emphasis was linked to the changing nature of society and of its relationship with industry. By the 1970s the market for furniture had become increasingly international. Styles changed very rapidly and marketing men were constantly in search of novelty. As in the past, mass market furniture continued to ape and adapt whatever was fashionable at the moment, and it had to respond quickly to new trends, as a larger sector of the public than ever before could afford to experiment freely with its tastes.

The sources of the new furniture movements of the 1970s and 1980s were highly diverse, and most of them were international. Some were specific to furniture, while others were part of more general cultural movements. One such general trend which had special implications for furniture was the so-called Crafts Revival – a phenomenon which grew out of the nostalgia of the late 1960s. Through the 1970s and 1980s it developed in Britain, the USA and a number of European countries – particularly Sweden and Denmark – into a fully-fledged movement.

There were two main strains to the revival of craftsmanship in furniture-making. One related to fine art, and the other to design. The former showed itself through a growing interest in furniture as sculpture. In the USA this was seen first in the work of men like Wharton Esherick and Wendell Castle, and, later, in that of the 'furniture-artists' of the 1980s, who included men like Howard Meister and Forrest Myers. In Britain artist-craftsmen like Floris van den Broecke, Fred Baier, and Eric de Graff blurred the distinctions between sculpture and furniture-making.

The craft revival on a more traditional level, relating to design,

A satin wood cabinet with a green burnished lacquer interior and ivory handles designed by John Makepeace and made by Andrew Whateley in 1980–2.

showed itself in the work of people such as Richard La Trobe Bateman, Alan Peters, and John Makepeace. They re-established the artisan-traditions of furniture-making rather in the manner of the 19th-century Arts and Crafts movement, although to different effect. Makepeace describes himself as a designer-craftsman. He trained as an apprentice and has worked, since the 1960s, in rare and expensive woods, creating exlusive, unique items displaying the techniques of fine workmanship to their best advantage. A double-sided desk from 1974, for instance, was made from macassar ebony, holly and buffalo suede with cedar draw linings and ivory handles, while a dining table from the same year was constructed out of harewood. On a more modest level, but with similar ideals, the designer-craftsman, David Colwell, moved to a small workshop in a Welsh valley in this period where he batch-produced a small folding chair made of ash and rattan.

A related concern of the 1970s and 1980s, expressed in a number of countries, was with dwindling world resources. The American design pundit, Victor Papanek, wrote a book entitled *Nomadic Furniture* which advocated a return to the vernacular tradition. The Scandinavians set out to put the theory into practice. In Sweden Johan Huldt and Jan Dranger designed a range of pieces for their

Johan Huldt and Jan Dranger's collapsible chair. It has a steel-tube frame and a removable cotton cover.

company, Innovator, using a bare minimum of materials. A writer in *Design* magazine explained that *"it was a demonstration of philosophical, if not political commitment at a time when young Scandinavians were fermenting debate about waste of materials, population increase and a newly-discovered ecology crisis."* The range, which comprized sofas, a coffee-table, a dinner trolley, a filing tray and a cot, were made of knockdown tubular steel frames (common to several of the pieces) covered with canvas which could be simply slipped on and off for easy maintenance. The pieces came packed flat in a cardboard box, ready to take away.

The sparse look of the Innovator range became characteristic of a

number of Scandinavian pieces in this period, most notable among them the Finnish chair designed by Simo Heikkala and Yrjo Wiherheimo for Vivero in the early 1980s. Finnish furniture had gone into a decline in the 1970s. The oil crisis had put an end to the plastic experiments of Eero Aarnio and Esko Pajamies for Asko, and the country didn't have the same craft traditions as Sweden and Denmark to fall back on. By the middle of the decade, however, it had become apparent that a new movement was emerging, headed by Yrjo Kukkapuro, which combined an interest in ergonomics with visual elegance. His chair designs (made of a variety of materials including wood, leather, steel and plastic) provided a spare yet elegant alternative to 'Italian chic'. By the end of the decade a number of small Finnish companies, among them Avarte and Vivero, had sprung up and a Finnish furniture renaissance was in full swing. Heikkala and Wiherheimo's chair for Vivero, called 'Verde' combined ergonomics, and visual simplicity with a minimal use of technology. It was assembled out of parts which could be made almost entirely by existing machine-tools, and what little tooling was needed was kept to a bare minimum. Only one compression mould, for instance, was required to manufacture the entire chair. This kind of sensitivity to resources underpinned a number of

A dining table and chairs from the mid 1980s in anodized aluminium designed by the American sculptor Forrest Myers and sold through a New York gallery called 'Furniture of the Twentieth-Century'.

the mass market.

One furniture style which became very popular in the 1970s but which had no avant-garde origins, was 'high-tech'. It was initially inspired by a book of that name written by two American critics (Joan Kron and Suzanne Slesin), which was published in the USA in 1978 and in Britain in the following year. It advocated the domestic use of materials and items originally destined for industrial purposes. Countless stores set up business, mostly in the USA, but also in Great Britain and Europe, specifically to sell cheap high-tech accessories to

Above: A chair from the early 1980s which combines Modernist and Post-Modernist details, by the Japanese designer Shigeru Uchida.

Finnish projects in these years. Even in Norway, a country which had no modern furniture tradition and which, compared with the other Scandinavian countries, had a low profile in modern furniture design, entered the field at this time with some highly innovative pieces, designed to help people's posture and prevent backaches and spinal disorders. Produced by the Westnofa and Håg companies, the range included a kneeling stool, a baby's high chair and a secretary's chair.

Ecology consciousness was only one feature of the 1970s. The mass market was more interested in style than philosophies. Improved communications meant that styles spread quickly from one country to another and they were quickly modified for

A 'High-Tech' interior, the components of which were designed by Ron Arad.

a young market, which used them to make an entire interior and to express a complete lifestyle. In sharp contrast with the stylistic revivals of the early decade, this was, above all, an optimistic, futuristic style which was both modern and cheap. Dexion book-cases; scaffolding supports for cupboards and beds; bulk-head and factory lights; car-seats; brightly-coloured metal storage racks; rubber flooring; metal and glass coffee-tables; and many other items combined to create an instant, total style which could be produced economically and created quickly in the home. It was an anti-designer style in as much as the pieces came, supposedly, 'ready-made', borrowed from industry. It served to break down the distinctions between traditional domestic furniture and furniture for the working environment. High-Tech furniture moved out of the office, the factory, the hospital, the café, and the market-place, into the home.

High-Tech had its roots in modern industry. The other radical development of the 1970s and 1980s to influence mass furniture was the Post-Modern movement, which reacted against industrialized culture. The name was originally applied to architecture, and was then used as an umbrella term to describe a whole range of furniture items produced in a number of countries – including Italy, the USA, Japan, Germany, France,

Britain and Finland. Broadly speaking, it rejected the production-oriented aspect of the Modern movement and embraced instead kitsch, popular culture, and the revival of period styles – often ironically.

The movement had its strongest and most articulate supporters in Italy, where the counter-designers of the 1960s re-emerged to lead a full-scale rejection of Italian chic and mass production furniture. In 1980 a writer in *Design* magazine noticed the presence, in Milan, of what he called 'a dramatic departure in taste' which he associated with the work of a design group called Studio Alchymia. It included Ettore Sottsass, Andrea Branzi (late of Archizoom), and Alexander Mendini (editor of *Domus*). Their furniture designs used industrial materials in bizarre shapes, covered in patterns. Most of them had distinct 1950s overtones.

The Viennese architect Hans Hollein's Post-Modern sofas designed for the Italian company Poltronova in 1984.

Paolo Deganello's little 'Artifici' coffee-tables designed for Cassina in the early 1980s.

In 1981, Memphis, a group furniture exhibition led by Ettore Sottass, took place in a gallery in Milan at the same time as the annual furniture fair. Its brightly-coloured, eclectic, densely-patterned pieces (including contributions from the American Post-Modern architect, Michael Graves, the Japanese architect Arata

The 'Torso' armchair, designed by Paolo Deganello for Cassina in 1982 owing much to furniture styles from the 1950s.

Ettore Sottsass' brightly coloured, plastic laminated cupboard designed for the 1981 Memphis exhibition in Milan.

Isozaki, and the Viennese architect Hans Hollein) shocked the Milanese design establishment to the core and renewed the debate about 'good design' in many countries. The enthusiastic press reaction to the Memphis experiment meant that, even though the pieces exhibited were only prototypes, it quickly became a model for many different countries. The groups that picked up the Memphis message included Totem in France and Poe Form in Japan. Even in Finland, Kukkapuro moved away, in 1982, from the minimal forms that had become the hallmark of his work,

to experiment with expressive shapes and bright colours.

In Italy the influence of what came to be called the 'New Design' was enormous in the couple of years after 1981. Cassina, for instance, launched a 1950s-inspired chair designed by Paolo Deganello – another of the 1960s generation of counter-designers. Zanotta commissioned Sottsass himself to design a couple of items for them; and Bieffeplast used the young designers attached to Sottsass, including Michele de Lucchi. The 1982 and 1983 Milan fairs were dominated by the Memphis furniture style – albeit modified somewhat for a mass audience – and it fed into a number of pieces in other countries as well. Most significantly it was a strong influence on student work in this period as it offered a fresh vision at a time when mainstream furniture was decidedly

dull. While never fully satisfying the brief of the 1960s counter-design movement, the New Design succeeded, nonetheless, in infiltrating the mass environment and in affecting a range of items from fashion to graphics, as well as furniture, in the process. It represented a rare instance, in this century, of furniture taking the lead in a cultural movement rather than following meekly behind architecture and technology.

In the USA Post-Modernism was much more clearly an architectural and interior design style than a cultural movement and the furniture that formed part of it was largely historical in inspiration. Another American phenomenon of these years was the habit of reviving 'Classic' items of modern furniture. This was an offshoot of the 'designer-furniture' movement, a marketing technique which owed much to the better

Richard Meier's range of furniture for Knoll from the early 1980s owes much to the work of Josef Hoffmann earlier this century.

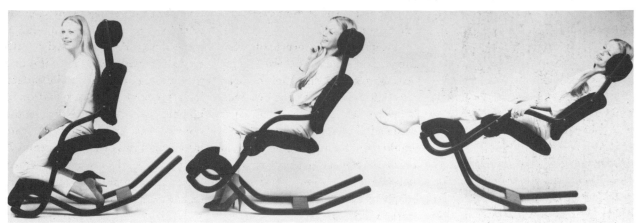

Above: Peter Opsvik's 'Tripos' chair from the early 1980s for the Norwegian Westnofa company which focuses on the problem of the sitter's posture

Below: Mario Bellini's 'Colonnata' table was designed for Cassina in 1977. The weight alone of the marble legs supports the top.

known 'designer-jeans' phenomenon. Knoll International had been the first American company to reproduce modern classics back in the 1950s beginning with a reproduction of a Mies van der Rohe design. In the mid 1960s the Italian company, Cassina, initiated its 'Master' series reproducing pieces by Le Corbusier, and, later, items by Rietveld, Mackintosh and, more recently, Gunnar Asplund. The American company, ICF, recently remade some furniture pieces designed by Eliel Saarinen, and Andre Puttman's Parisian company, Ecart, has revived a number of pieces by René Herbst, Eileen Gray, and Mallet-Stevens, from the 1920s. This reproducing of 'classics' has become a strong force in the 1980s, a decade which has no strong style of its own, and which needs instant status symbols, in the form of modern designs which have proved their worth by the test of time. In an age of diversity and untested values it is safer, in many ways, to revive the past. Inevitably this tendency is moving further down market, although at these levels it is expressed less in accurate reproductions than in vague stylistic evocations of the original. This was well demonstrated by the inclusion of a Hoffmannesque piece (Josef Hoffmann is the most popular of the recently much revived Viennese designers from the turn of the century) on the stand of a British mass manufacturing company at a recent fair.

A controversial American experiment with Post-Modern furniture was the introduction, by Knoll International, of a range designed by the architect Robert Venturi. The ideas he outlined in his book *Complexity and Contradiction in Architecture*, heralded the Post-Modern architectural movement. His new furniture pieces are sophisticated, intellectual exercises reintroducing the concept of 'diversity in unity' into furniture production. As a fashionable furniture style, Post-Modernism had begun to fade by the mid 1980s and was replaced by an elegant Neo-Modernism best exemplified by the work of the Frenchman Philippe Starck – who brought domestic furniture back into the headlines when he decorated a room in President Mitterand's residence.

In the mid 1980s there are still many furniture styles available to choose from. While the large-scale furniture industry has not picked up during the recession, it has more or less survived and has been joined by a parallel system of small-scale enter-prises, led by designers, marketing men and entrepreneurs, in many countries. Together with fashion, fur-niture has increasingly become one of our essential status symbols. As the mass consumption of style comes to dominate the age we live in, the con-sumer has a stronger influence than ever before on the appearance of mass-produced furniture.

Sofas, armchair and a coffee-table designed by Ettore Sottsass for Knoll International in 1984 – an instance of 'radical' design penetrating the furniture mainstream.

An interior furnished by the British retail outlet 'Next Interiors' illustrating the stylistic eclecticism of the 1980s.

The Japanese designer, Toshiyuki Kita's playful Mickey Mouse-inspired chair for Cassina called 'Wink', designed in the early 1980s.

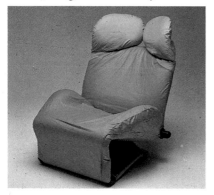

CONCLUSION

"Galloping furniturization may be diagnosed as an intolerable tension between culture and technology. Pure technology would probably bring furniture to an end, or at least render it invisible."

Reyner Banham *The Chair as Art* 1970

AS this book has been at pains to show, Banham's 'intolerable tension' lies right at the heart of domestic furniture in this century. Many of the objects around us bear direct testimony to it. Countless hi-fi sets and television consoles, for instance, still bear the last traces of the 'furniturization' process. Their 'wood-effect' plastic laminate surfaces show how they are torn between being items of furniture or pieces of equipment. In contrast, the all-metal chair has identified itself with 20th-century technological life. It has more in common with a piece of Japanese electronic equipment than with a conventional upholstered sofa.

The division between furniture and equipment or, in Banham's words, 'between culture and technology' is not clear-cut, but the desire to emphasize both alternatives can be seen in contemporary furniture designs. They are both repeatedly expressed, at different moments, by mass-produced, domestic furniture in this century. As Banham has explained, and as the Archigram group also pointed out in the mid 1960s pure technology, followed to its logical end, would have eliminated the horsehair sofa and the kitchen dresser years ago. We could just as easily all be sitting on lumps of polyurethane foam and storing our kitchen equipment in concealed, built-in cupboards. The fact that so many furniture habits, types and styles have remained with us for centuries bears witness to the fact that, in the end, social, psychological and cultural forces determine what types of furniture most people live with for most of their lives.

Nonetheless, there has also been a strong technological pull in modern furniture. Experiments with new materials and manufacturing techniques have produced some of this century's most familiar items, from the plywood-backed wardrobe, to the chipboard storage unit, to the metal-legged kitchen table, to the trolley with its plastic laminated surface. The cheapness and efficiency of these advances has meant that modern furniture is no longer a luxury, available only for a few, but a basic necessity for most people in the industrialized world. Up until the 1960s, the major furniture breakthroughs of this century all depended, in one way or another, upon technological advances.

As this book has also made clear, however, the mass taste for furniture in this century has been conservative rather than the innovatory, and many people have preferred, and still prefer, to live with reproduction or old pieces rather than with new, modern-styled items. In general, society has resisted the argument of many architects in this century that furniture can, and should, be integrated into the room structure in the same way as bathroom equipment. Even more than the house itself, domestic furniture has refused to be reduced to an efficient machine. However persuasive the argument that greater efficiency leads to improved living standards, it has met with continued resistance. The war-time Utility scheme in Britain, for example, and the numerous attempts made after the War to impose strict measurements on furniture, never took a total hold on the market.

Furniture enhances most of the leisure activities of the home, from eating to sleeping, relaxing, entertaining, reading or watching television. There is of course a level of efficiency needed in the home, particularly for purposes such as storage and cleaning, and obviously the size of domestic furniture must fit the living space. But, whereas at work efficiency is the key word for furniture, at home it is just one of the many qualities required.

The demands we make of domestic furniture are many and varied, and the ideal formula is, of course, impossible to achieve. This century has seen both its symbolic and its practical roles come under close scrutiny, and various solutions suggested for each. Several major pendulum swings have occurred. During the first 30 years of the century, the 'machine aesthetic' dominated most developments in modern furniture. The following decade focused on turning modern machines, like radios and gramophones, back into furniture. In the 1960s it looked as if furniture was going to be seduced back into the sphere of equipment, but once again it resisted that pull, returning instead to the more reassuring framework of traditional values.

For all these, and many more reasons, domestic furniture is one of the richest elements in our material environment. It is part both of our heritage and of our everyday surroundings, and it seems likely that it will always continue to play an essential role in our society and our culture.

A radio divan bed combining a cocktail cabinet, book-case, telephone, clock, and radio set was displayed at the Radio Exhibition at Olympia in 1934.

BIBLIOGRAPHY

AGIUS, P. *British Furniture 1880-1915* Antique Collectors Club, Woodbridge 1978

AKERBLOM, B. *Standing and Sitting Posture* A.B. Nordiska Bokhandeln, Stockholm 1948.

ALOI, R. *Esempi di Arredamenti Moderno* Hoepli, Milan 1957.

AMBASZ, E. (ed) *Italy: the New Domestic Landscape* Museum of Modern Art, New York 1972.

ASLIN, E. *Nineteenth-Century English Furniture* Faber, London 1962

ASLIN, E. *The Aesthetic Movement* Ferndale Editions, London 1981

BATLEY, H.W. *A Series of Studies for Domestic Furniture and Decoration* Studio, London 1883.

BAYNES, K&K *Gordon Russell* Design Council, London 1980

BERMPOHL, R. & WINKELMANN, H. *Das Möbelbuch* C. Bertelsman, Gutersloh 1958.

BISHOP, R. *Centuries and Styles of the American Chair 1640-1970* Harper, New York 1972

BOLTENSTERN, E. *Wiener Möbel* Julius Hoffman, Stuttgart 1935

BONNETT, D. *Contemporary Cabinet design and Construction* Batsford, London 1956.

BRANZI, A & De LUCCHI, M. *Il Design Italiano degli Anni '50* I.G.I.S., Milan 1981.

BUTTREY, D.N. *Plastics in the Furniture Industry* Macdonald, London 1964.

CAMPBELL-COLE, B. & BENTON, T. (eds) *Tubular Steel Furniture* The Art Book Company, London 1979.

CAPLAN, R. *The Design of Herman Miller* Whitney, New York 1976.

CARRINGTON, N. *Design and Decoration in the Home* Batsford, London 1952.

CATHERS, D.M. *Furniture of the American Arts and Crafts Movement* New American Libray New York 1981.

CONWAY, H. *Ernest Race* Design Council, London 1982.

DARLING, S. *Chicago furniture: Art, Craft and Industry 1833-1983* W.W. Norton and Company , New York/London 1984.

De FUSCO, R. *Le Corbusier, Designer, Furniture* Rizzoli, New York 1979

DAL FABRO, M. *Furniture for Modern Interiors* Reinhold, New York 1954.

DAL FABRO, M. *Modern Furniture: its Design and Construction* Reinhold, New York 1958.

DITZEL, N & J. *Danish Chairs* Host and Sons, Copenhagen 1954.

DOMERGUE, D. *Artists Design Furniture* Harry N. Abrams, New York 1985.

DREXLER, A. *Charles Eames: Furniture from the Design Collection* Museum of Modern Art, New York 1973.

FAIRBANKS, J. and BATES, E.B. *American Furniture 1620 to the Present.*

FALES, W. *What's New in Home Decorating?* Dodd, Mead and Company, New York 1936.

FOSSATI, P. *Il Design in Italia 1945-1972* Einaudi, Milan 1972.

FRANKL, P. *New Dimensions* Brewer and Warren Inc, New York 1936.

FREY, G. *The Modern Chair: 1850 to today* Tiranti, London 1970.

GARNER, P. *Twentieth-Century Furniture* Phaidon, Oxford 1980

GIEDION, S. *Mechanization Takes Command* W.W.Norton, New York 1948.

GLAESER, L. *Ludwig Mies van der Rohe: Furniture and Furniture Drawings from the Design Collection* Museum of Modern Art, New York 1977.

GLOAG, J. *British Furniture-Makers* Collins, London 1945.

GLOAG, J. *The Englishman's Chair* Allen and Unwin, London 1964.

GOLDFINGER, E. *British Furniture Today* Tiranti, London 1951.

GRIEF, M. *Depression Modern: The Thirties Style in America* Universe, New York 1975.

HAMILTON, N. (ed) *Svensk Form* Design Council, London 1981.

HAMISH FRASER, W. *The Coming of the Mass Market 1850-1914* Macmillan, London 1981.

HANKS, D. *Innovative Furniture in America from 1800 to the present* Horizon Press,

New York 1981.

HANKS, D. *The Decorative Designs of Frank Lloyd Wright* Academy Editions, London 1979.

HATJE, G. (ed) *Neue Mobel, New Furniture 1954* Halze, Stuttgart 1954.

HENNESSEY, W.J. *Russel Wright: American Designer* M.I.T. Press, New York 1983.

HIORT, E. *Modern Danish Furniture* Architectural Book Publishing Company, New York 1956.

HJORTH, H. *Machine Woodworking* The Bruce Publishing Company, Milwaukee 1947.

HOOPER, J. and R. *Modern Furniture and Fittings* Batsford, London 1948.

HUNTER, G.L. *Home Furnishing* John Lane Company, New York 1913.

JERVIS, S. *Victorian Furniture* Ward Lock, London 1968.

JOEL, D. *Furniture Design Set Free* Dent, London 1973.

KRON, J and SLESIN, S. *High-Tech: The Industrial Style and Source Book for the Home* Allen Lane, New York 1978.

LEONARDI, S. *Produzione a Consumo dei Mobile per abitazione in Italia* Fetrinelli, Milan 1959.

LOGIE, G. *Furniture from Machines* Allen and Unwin,

London 1948.

LUCIE-SMITH, E. *Furniture: A Concise History* Thames and Hudson, London, 1979.

LYALL, S. *Hille: 75 Years of British Furniture* Elron Press, London 1981.

LYNES, R. *The Taste-Makers: The Shaping of American Popular Taste* Dover Publications Inc. New York 1949.

McFADDEN, D. (ed) *Scandinavian Modern Design 1880-1980* Harry N. Abrams, New York 1983.

MAGNUSSEN, C. *The Modern Chair: Its Origins and Evolution* La Jolla Museum of Contemporary Art, California 1977.

MALMSTEN, C. *Swedish Furniture: Schwedische Mobel* Wipl, Basel 1954.

MANG, K. *History of Modern Furniture* Academy Editions, London 1979.

MAYES, L.T. *The History of Chair-Making in High Wycombe* Routledge and Kegan Paul, London 1960.

MEADMORE, C. *The Modern Chair: Classics in Production* Studio Vista, New York 1975.

MIESTAMO, R. *The Form and Substance of Finnish Furniture* Askon Saätiö, Lahti 1981.

MOODY, E. *Modern Furniture* Studio Vista, London 1966.

NELSON, G. *Chairs* Whitney, New York 1953.

NELSON, G. and WRIGHT, H. *Tomorrow's House* Simon and Schuster, New York 1945.

OLIVER, J.L. *The Development and Structure of the Furniture Industry* Pergamon, Oxford 1966.

PAGE, M. *Furniture designed by Architects* Whitney, New York 1980.

PATMORE, D. *Colour Schemes and Modern Furnishing* The Studio, London/New York 1945.

PERRY, T.D. *Modern Plywood* Harper, New York 1942.

PEVSNER, N. *An Enquiry into Industrial Art in England* Cambridge University Press, London 1937.

PILE, J.F. *Modern Furniture* John Wiley and Sons, New York 1979

PRITCHARD, J. *View from a Long Chair* Routledge and Kegan Paul, London 1984.

PRUS, T. and DAWSON, D. *A New Design for Living* Lane Publications, London 1982.

RITTER, E (ed) *Italian Design: Furniture* Einandi, Milan and Rome 1968.

ROBERTSON, H. *Reconstruction and the Home* Batsford, London 1947.

ROBSJOHN-GIBBINGS, T.H. *Goodbye Mr. Chippendale* Harper, New York 1947.

ROSENTHAL, R. and RATZKA, H.L. *The Story of Modern Applied Art* Harper New York 1948.

RUSSELL, F., GARNER, P. and READ, J. *A Century of Chair Design 1850-1950* Academy Editions, London 1980.

RUSSELL, G. *Looking at Furniture* Lund Humphries, London 1964.

SANTINI, P.C. *The Years of Italian Design? A Portrait of Cesare Cassina* Electa, Milan 1981.

SCHNECK, A.G. *Neue Mobel von Jugendstil bis heute* Bruckmann, Munich 1962.

SEGERSTAD, U. Hard af. *Modern Scandinavian Furniture* Studio, London 1963.

SEMBACH, K. *Contemporary Furniture* Design Council, London 1982.

SIRONEN, M.K. *A History of American Furniture* N.I. Bredenstock, Pennsylvania 1936.

WEAVER, L. *High Wycombe Furniture* Fanfare Press, London 1929.

WELLS, P.A. *Furniture for Small Houses* Batsford, London 1920.

WILK, C. *Marcel Breuer: Furniture and Interiors* The Museum of Modern Art, New York 1981.

WILK, C. *Thonet: 150 Years of Furniture* The Museum of Modern Art, New York, 1980.

WRIGHT, L. *Warm and Snug: The History of the Bed* Routledge, London 1962.

YOUNG, D. and YOUNG, B. *Furniture in Britain Today* Tiranti, London 1964.

Articles

AMES, K.L. 'Grand Rapids Furniture at the Time of the Centennial' in Quimby, I.M.G. *Winterthur Portfolio* 10. Charlottesville 1975.

BANHAM, R. 'The Chair as Art' in *Modern Chairs 1918-1970* London 1970.

BENTON, T. 'Backgrounds to the Bauhaus' in Faulkner, T. (ed). *Design 1900-1960* Newcastle 1976.

CROWTHER, J. 'Surveys of Industry: Furniture' in *Design* London, March 1962.

DUNNETT, H. McG. 'Furniture Since the War' in *Architectural Review* London March 1951.

DUNNETT, H.McG. 'packaged Furniture' in *Architectural Review* London April 1952.

EARL, P.A. 'Craftsmen and Machines: The Nineteenth-Century Furniture Industry' in Quimby, I.M.G. (ed) *Technological Innovation and the Decorative Arts* Charlottesville 1974.

JULIUS, L. 'The Furniture Industry' in *Journal of the Royal Society of*

Arts London May 1967

KAUFMANN, E. 'Finn Juhl of Copenhagen' in *Interiors* New York November 1953

JOHNSTON, D. 'Upholstery: A Survey' in *Design* London, July 1959

MANSER, J. 'Free-form Furniture' in *Design* London December 1968

McGRATH, R. 'New Materials, New Methods' in *Architectural Review* London June 1930

MORTON SHAND, R. 'Timber as a Reconstructed Material' in *Architectural Review* London February 1936

NELSON, G. 'The Furniture Industry' in *Fortune* New York January 1947

NELSON, G. 'Modern Furniture' in *Interiors* New York July 1949

PEVSNER, N. 'The Evolution of the Easy Chair' in *Architectural Review* London March 1942

PEVSNER, N. 'Plywood' in *Architectural Review* London September 1939

RUSSELL, G. 'Furniture' in *Design '46* London 1946

THOMAS, M.H. 'Unit Furniture, Built-in Furniture and Modular Coordination' in *Design* London August 1954

WILSON, R.C. 'Chair Design in the Twentieth-Century' In Faulkner. T. (ed) *Design 1900–1960* Newcastle 1976

YAKOBSON, L.N. 'Standard Furniture' in *Design For Today* London September 1935

Unpublished PhD thesis

WORDEN, S. *Furniture for the Living-Room: An Investigation of the Interaction between Society, Industry and Design in Britain from 1919–1939* Brighton Polytechnic 1980

Exhibition Catalogues

London: Geffrye Museum. *CC41: Utility Furniture and fashion 1941–1951* 1974

London: Whitechapel Art Gallery. *Setting Up Home for Bill and Betty* 1952

London: Whitechapel Art Gallery. *Modern Chairs 1818–1970* 1970

New York: Metropolitan Museum of Art. *Design in America: The Cranbrook Vision 1925–1950* 1983

New York: Whitney Museum of American Art. *Shape and Environment: Furniture by American Architects* 1982

ACKNOWLEDGEMENTS

T = top; B = bottom; R = right; L = left

The author and publishers would like to thank the following for their kind permission to reproduce the photographs on the pages listed: Franco Albini: pages 66, 67; Karl Andersson & Soner: page 61; Ron Arad: page 100B; Aram Designs: pages 31T, B, 77; Arflex: page 69; Artek: page 37T, B; Artemide: cover (UK edition); Asko Oy: pages 36, 65, 89T, BL; Avarte Oy: title page; B & B Italia: pages 93B, 96T, 97; Batsford: pages 80BR, 81; BBC Hulton Picture Library: pages 46, 87B, 106; Bowman Bros. Ltd: page 47; British Architectural Library: page 39; Cassina Spa: pages 28, 71, 93T, 101T, BR, 103B, 104BL; Chicago Historical Society: page 41; Christie's: page 13T; Sheridan Coakley: page 8; The Design Council: pages 40T, 48, 50B, TR, 51, 69B, 73, 74, 80BL, 85, 87T, 88B, 90, 96B; page 43 reprinted from WHAT'S NEW IN HOME DECORATING by Winnifred Fales by permission of the publishers Dodd, Mead & Co., Inc.; Dux Interiors Ltd: page 33B; D D Flicker: page 101BL; Form Program AB: page 99; Habitat: page 27; Fritz Hansen: pages 62B, 63T; Johannes Hansen: page 62T; Heal and Sons: page 76T; Horizon Press: page 23 reprinted from INNOVATIVE FURNITURE IN AMERICA: From 1800 to the Present by David A. Hanks, copyright 1981, by permission of the publishers Horizon Press, New York; Knoll International: pages 55, 57T, 59, 83, 102B, 104T; Liberty Retail Ltd: page 15B; John Makepeace: page 98; Herman Miller, Inc: pages 40, 53, 56T, B, 57B, 58; Forrest Myers: page 100TL; Next Interiors: page 104BR; W. W. Norton & Co, Inc: pages 20, 42, OMK: page 89BR; Parker-Knoll: page 50TR; Poltronova: page 119; J. Pritchard: page 51; Race Furniture Ltd: pages 76B, 78, 79T, 85; Ettore Sottsass: page 102T; The Studio Ltd: page 49; The Studio Magazine: page 15T; Superstudio: page 95; Tecno: page 69T; Thonet: pages 11, 19, 33T; The Trustees of the Victoria and Albert Museum: pages 13B, 14, 61, 68, 79, 80T, 88T; Hans J. Wegner: page 62T; Westminster City Libraries Archives Department: page 15B; Westnofa Furniture: page 103T; Zanotta Spa: pages 30, 72, 94, 96B.

INDEX